NAMES OF GOD

NATHAN STONE

MOODY PRESS

CHICAGO

Copyright, 1944, by
THE MOODY BIBLE INSTITUTE
OF CHICAGO

ISBN: 0-8024-5854-8

35 37 39 40 38 36 34

Printed in the United States of America

CONTENTS

PRONUNCIATION OF NAMES OF GOD

Elohim	el-lo-heem′
Jehovah	je-ho′-vah
Adonai	a-do-ni′
El-Shaddai	el shad-di′
Jehovah-jireh	je-ho′-vah yeer′-eh
Jehovah-rophe	je-ho′-vah ro′-phay
Jehovah-nissi	je-ho′-vah nis-see
Jehovah-M'Kaddesh	je-ho′-vah m′-kad′-desh
Jehovah-shalom	je-ho′-vah shal-lom′
Jehovah-tsidkenu	je-ho′-vah tsid-kay′-noo
Jehovah-rohi	je-ho′-vah ro′-ee
Jehovah-shammah	je-ho′-vah sham′-mah

INTRODUCTION

THE CHAPTERS contained in this volume were given originally as a course in the Radio School of the Bible over WMBI, Chicago. A number of requests for their appearance in a more permanent form, and the fact that comparatively little is written upon a subject worthy of more interest and attention, have led to their publication.

It has been the writer's purpose to show not only the significance of the names of God in the Old Testament, but that they find their complement and fulfillment in the person and work of the Lord Jesus Christ in the New—He who is the effulgence of the glory and the image of the substance of Jehovah, and in whom "dwelleth all the fullness of the Godhead bodily."

The writer acknowledges a measure of indebtedness to such works as those of Webb-Peploe, Andrew Jukes, R. B. Girdlestone, and Parkhurst's *Hebrew Lexicon*.

The Scripture quotations are from the King James Version and the American Standard Version (A.S.V.), while some are free translations from the Hebrew.

This little volume goes forth with the hope and prayer that we may better know Him whose name is above every name, and that some may find in Him that name apart from which "there is none other name under heaven given among men, whereby we must be saved."

1

ELOHIM

THE FIRST QUESTION in some of our catechisms is, "What is the chief end of man?" and the answer is, "Man's chief end is to glorify God and to enjoy Him forever." But we will experience God in such fashion— we will glorify Him and enjoy Him—only in proportion as we know Him. The knowledge of God is more essential for the Christian, and indeed for all the world, than the knowledge of anything else—yes, of all things together. The prayer of the Lord Jesus for His disciples in John 17:3 was: "And this is life eternal that they should know thee the only true God, and him whom thou didst send, even Jesus Christ" (A.S.V.). And speaking of this, Christ, our Jehovah-Jesus, Paul sums up in Philippians 3:10 the great goal of his life: "That I may know him."

"I suppose if sin had not entered the world," says one writer, "the acquisition of the knowledge of God would have been the high occupation of man forever and ever." It is for a lack of knowledge of God that the prophet Hosea informs his people they are destroyed. And it is from the lack of knowledge of God that many are without spiritual power or life. There is little real knowledge in these days of the one, true God.

There are many ways, of course, in which we may study God. The God who of old time spoke, "unto the fathers in the prophets by divers portions and in divers manners, hath at the end of these days spoken to us in his Son," the epistle to the Hebrews tells us. And this Son, Jesus Christ, while on earth said in the great discourse and prayer with God: "I have manifested thy name unto the men which thou gavest me out of the world . . ." (John 17:6). "And I have declared unto them thy name, and will declare it: that the love wherewith thou hast loved me may be in them, and I in them (John 17:26).

True, it is in the face of Jesus Christ we best see the glory of God; yet while we are in the flesh we can only know in part at most. And it behooves us to know all we can learn of God. All the Scriptures are profitable to us for instruction and edification, but perhaps not very many people know much about the person of God as revealed in His names. Surely a study of these names should be a most profitable way of increasing that knowledge.

When Moses received a commission from God to go to His oppressed people in Egypt and deliver them from bondage, he said: "When I come unto the children of Israel, and shall say unto them, The God of your fathers hath sent me unto you; and they shall say to me, What is his name? what shall I say unto them?" (Exod. 3:13).

Now the word *God* or even *Lord,* as we see it in our English Bibles, conveys little more to us than the designation of the Supreme Being and Sovereign of the universe. It tells little about His character and ways. Indeed we cannot say all that the mysterious word *God* means to us until we know more about Him. And we can know little of what the word *God* means until we go to the language from which the word *God* is translated, the language which is the first written record of the revelation of Himself, the language in which He spoke to Moses and the prophets.

Missionaries and translators have always had difficulty in finding a suitable word for the Hebrew word we translate God. Those who have attempted to translate this word into Chinese, for instance, have always been divided and still are as to which word is best. One of the greatest of these translations preferred a word which means "Lord of Heaven."

Now a name in the Old Testament was often an indication of a person's character or of some peculiar quality. But what one name could be adequate to God's greatness? After all, as one writer declares, a name imposes some limitation. It means that an object or person is this and not that, is here and not there. And if the Heaven of heavens cannot contain God, how can a name describe Him? What a request of Moses, then, that was —that the infinite God should reveal Himself to finite man by any one name! We can hardly understand or appreciate Moses himself unless we see him in his many-sided character of learned man and shepherd, leader and legislator, soldier and statesman, impulsive, yet meekest of men. We can know David, too, not only as shepherd, warrior, and king, but also as a prophet, a poet, and musician.

Even so, the Old Testament contains a number of names and compound names for God which reveal Him in some aspect of His character and dealings with mankind. It is our purpose in this series of studies to examine these names and their meanings, their significance for ourselves as well as for those of old.

As one would expect, the opening statement of the

Scriptures contains the name *God*. "In the beginning God!" The Hebrew word from which this word *God* is translated is Elohim. While not the most frequently occurring word for the Deity, it occurs 2,570 times. The one which occurs most frequently is the word in the King James Version translated Lord, and in the American Standard Version, Jehovah.

Elohim occurs in the first chapter of Genesis thirty-two times. After that, the name Jehovah appears as well as Elohim; and in many places a combination of the two—Jehovah-Elohim. As far back as the twelfth century students noticed that these different names were used in the Bible, but thought little of it until about the eighteenth century when a French physician thought he discovered the reason for the use of different names of God. He said that the Book of Genesis (especially) was based on two other documents, one written by a man who had apparently known God only as Elohim—this was called the Elohistic document—and the other written by a man who had known God only by the name Jehovah—this was called the Jehovistic document.

Scholars pursued this theory until they thought there had originally been five or six documents, and even many fragments of documents all pieced and fitted together by a later editor, and then altered and added to by still later editors so that some of the stories we now read in Genesis and other books were made up of parts of stories from various documents and fragments. Moses was denied authorship of most of the Pentateuch. The theory was carried to such lengths of absurdity that it was far more difficult to believe than the simple, plain declaration of the Bible itself that Moses wrote these things. And indeed who, of all people, could have been in a better position and better able to write them than he? One can only think of many of these scholars that much learning hath made them mad. The point is that they could see no other basis, no other significance for the use of different names for God in the Old Testament than a literary basis—a literary significance— which is no significance at all for the spiritual mind. There is a spiritual significance in the use of these different names. It is much more "rational" to believe that the great and infinite and eternal God has given us these different names to express different aspects of His being and the different relationships He sustains to His creatures.

THE MEANING OF THE WORD

In order to gain some idea of the meaning of this name of God, Elohim, we must examine its origin and note how, generally, it is used. There is some difference of opinion as to the root from which Elohim is derived. Some hold to the view that it is derived from the shorter word *El*, which means mighty, strong, prominent. This word *El* itself is translated "God" some 250 times and frequently in circumstances which especially indicate the great power of God. For instance, in Numbers 23:22 God is spoken of as the El who brought Israel up out of Egypt—"he hath as it were the strength of an unicorn" (wild ox). The Scriptures make very much of God's mighty arm in that great deliverance. So in the next verse follows: "it shall be said of Jacob and Israel, what hath God [El] wrought."

In Deuteronomy 10:17 we read that "Jehovah your Elohim is God of gods, and Lord of lords, *the God or*

El who is great, mighty, and dreadful." It is this word *El* which is used in that great name *Almighty God,* the name under which God made great and mighty promises to Abraham and to Jacob (Gen. 17:1; 35:11). It is also one of the names given to that promised Son and Messiah of Isaiah 9:6, 7—God, the Mighty.

Thus, from this derivation, Elohim may be said to express the general idea of greatness and glory. In the name *Jehovah,* as we shall see more fully, are represented those high moral attributes of God which are displayed only to rational creatures. The name *Elohim,* however, contains the idea of creative and governing power, of omnipotence and sovereignty. This is clearly indicated by the fact that from Genesis 1:1 to 2:4 the word *Elohim* alone is used, and that thirty-five times. It is the Elohim who by His mighty power creates the vast universe; who says, and it is done; who brings into being what was not; by whose word the worlds were framed so that things which are seen were not made of the things which do appear (Heb. 11:3). It is this Elohim with whose Greek equivalent Paul confronts the philosophers on Mars' hill saying that He made the world (cosmos) and all things, and by this very fact is constituted possessor and ruler of heaven and earth; whose presence cannot be confined by space; whose power doesn't need man's aid, for through His great will and power and agency all things and nations have their very being.

It is most appropriate that by this name God should reveal Himself—bringing cosmos out of chaos, light out of darkness, habitation out of desolation, and life in His image.

There is another word from which some say Elohim

is derived. It is *Alah,* which is said to mean to declare or to swear. Thus it is said to imply a covenant relationship. Before examining this derivation, however, it may be well to say that in either case, whether El or Alah, the idea of omnipotence in God is expressed. To make a covenant implies the power and right to do so, and it establishes the fact of "absolute authority in the Creator and Ruler of the universe." So the Elohim is seen making a covenant with Abraham, and because there is none greater He swears by Himself. "By myself I have sworn." In Genesis 17 we see perhaps a combination of both of these derivations. In verse 1 we have: "I am the Almighty God [El-Shaddai]; walk before me, and be thou perfect"; in verse 7: "I will establish my covenant between me and thee and thy seed after thee in their generations for an everlasting covenant, to be to thee Elohim and to thy seed after thee"—that is, to be with them in covenant relationship.

It is the Elohim who says to Noah, "The end of all flesh is come before me." But He cannot completely destroy the work of His hands concerning which He has made a covenant and so He continues: "But with thee will I establish my covenant" (Gen. 6:18). "And the bow shall be in the cloud; and I will look upon it, that I may remember the everlasting covenant between God and every living creature of all flesh . . . and the waters shall no more become a flood to destroy all flesh" (Gen. 9:16, 15).

The Elohim remembers Abraham when He destroys the cities of the plain and for His covenant's sake spares Lot. Joseph on his deathbed declares to his brethren: "I die; but *Elohim* will surely visit you, and bring you up out of this land unto the land which he sware to Abraham, to Isaac, and to Jacob" (Gen. 50:24). He is the Elohim who keeps covenant and lovingkindness with His servants who walk before Him with all their heart (I Kings 8:23).

With regard to Israel, over and over again it is written: "I shall be unto you for Elohim and ye shall be unto me for a people." The covenant element in this name is clearly seen because of God's covenant relationship to Israel, and this is especially brought out in such a passage as Jeremiah 31:33 and 32:40, where the name *Elohim* is used in connection with that new covenant, an everlasting covenant which God will one day make with His people Israel when He will put His law and His fear within their hearts.

To Israel in distress comes the word: "Comfort ye, comfort ye, my people, said your Elohim" (Isa. 40:1). For the eternal God who covenants for and with them and us will keep His covenant.

THE PLURAL FORM

There is one other striking peculiarity in the name *Elohim*. It is in the plural. It has the usual Hebrew ending for all masculine nouns in the plural. A devout saint and Hebrew scholar of two centuries ago, Dr. Parkhurst,[1] defined the word *Elohim* as a name usually given in the Scriptures to the ever blessed Trinity by which they represent themselves as under the obligation of an oath to perform certain conditions. According to this

---

[1] Parkhurst, *Hebrew Lexicon—See* Elohim.

definition the Elohim covenanted not only with the creation but, as the Godhead, within itself, concerning the creation. This is seen from Psalm 110, where David says concerning his Lord, the coming anointed One or Messiah: "The Lord hath sworn, and will not repent, Thou art a priest forever after the order of Melchizedek." This is, of course, as the Book of Hebrews confirms, the Lord Jesus Christ, the Lamb slain from the foundation of the world, the first and the last, the eternally begotten Son of God, the object of God's love before the foundation of the world (John 17:24); who shared God's glory before the world was (John 17:5). Colossians 1:16 tells us that by Him or in Him were all things created. But creation is the act of the Elohim. Therefore, Christ is in the Elohim or Godhead. Then even in Genesis 1:3 we read that the spirit of the Elohim moved or brooded over the face of the waters. The entire creation, animate and inanimate, was, then, not only the work of the Elohim, but the object of a covenant within the Elohim guaranteeing its redemption and perpetuation. It is quite clear that the Elohim is a plurality in unity. So, Dr. Parkhurst continues: "Accordingly Jehovah is at the beginning of creation called Elohim, which implies that the divine persons had sworn when they created."[2]

It is significant that although plural in form it is constantly accompanied by verbs and adjectives in the singular. In the very first verse of Genesis the verb *create* is singular, and so all through the chapter and indeed through the Bible. In many places (as in Deut. 32:39; Isa. 45:5, 22, etc.) we find singular pronouns. "I am Elohim and there is no Elohim beside *me*." Other places

---

[2] *Ibid.*

in the Scriptures (II Kings 19:4, 16; Ps. 7:9; 57:2, etc.) use adjectives in the singular with Elohim. In contrast with this, when the word *elohim* is used of heathen gods, plural adjectives are used, as in I Samuel 4:8, etc. Then again this one Elohim speaks of Himself as *Us,* as in Genesis 1:26, "Let us make man in our image"; in Genesis 3:22, which speaks of man becoming like one of us; in 11:7 God says: "Let us go down and confound their language." In Genesis 35:7 Jacob builds an altar at Bethel, calling it El Beth-El, the God of the House of God because there the Elohim revealed themselves to him. Ecclesiastes 12:1 is rather, "Remember thy Creators"—plural, not singular. To the sovereign Lord of the universe, the Jehovah of hosts, whom Isaiah saw exalted high upon a throne, is ascribed the threefold Holy, and that same One from the throne calls to the prophet, "Whom shall I send and who will go for us?" So instances could be multiplied.

There are some who object to the idea of the Trinity in the word *Elohim,* and it is only fair to say that some conservative scholars as well as liberal and critical would not agree with it, among them John Calvin. They say that the plural is only a plural of majesty such as used by rulers and kings. But such use of the plural was not known then. We find no king of Israel speaking of himself as "we" and "us." Besides, the singular pronoun is so often used with Elohim. To be consistent with that view we should always find not *"I am your Elohim,"* as we do find, but *"We are your Elohim."*[3]

Others call it the plural of intensity and argue that the Hebrews often expressed a word in the plural to

---

[3] Girdlestone, *Old Testament Synonyms,* p. 39.

give it a stronger meaning—so blood, water, life are expressed in the plural. But as one writer points out,[4] these arguments only favor the idea of a Trinity in the Elohim. The use of the plural only implies (even in the plural of majesty) "that the word in the singular is not full enough to set forth all that is intended." With Elohim the plural form teaches us that no finite word can adequately convey the idea of the infinite personality or the unity of persons in the Godhead.

Certainly the use of this word in the plural is wonderfully consistent with that great and precious doctrine of the Trinity, and its use as already shown in the Old Testament surely must confirm that view.

There is blessing and comfort in this great name of God signifying supreme power, sovereignty, and glory on the one hand, for "thine [Elohim] is the power and the kingdom and the glory"; and on the other hand signifying a covenant relationship which He is ever faithful to keep. Thus He says to us, "I will be to you a God" (Elohim), and we may say, "My God [Elohim]; in him will I trust" (Ps. 91:2).

---

[4] *Ibid.*

2

JEHOVAH

IN THE AUTHORIZED or King James Version of our Bible the Hebrew word *Jehovah* is translated "LORD" in capitals to distinguish it from another Hebrew word, *Adonai,* also translated Lord. The Hebrew word is transliterated Jehovah in the American Standard Version. Jehovah is the name by far the most frequently employed in the Old Testament, occurring 6,823 times. It appears for the first time in Genesis 2:4, here together with Elohim as Jehovah-Elohim, and so all through the second and third chapters, except in the story of the temptation where only the name *Elohim* appears. After this we find the name of Jehovah alone, or Jehovah and Elohim together, or sometimes we find the two names used separately even in one sentence. This makes it difficult for those critics who would tell us that wherever the names *Jehovah* and *Elohim* appear separately they come from different documents, for it is incongruous to conceive of a later writer who took bits of different documents to put together even one sentence.

For example, Jacob in his dream at Beth-El hears the voice of God saying: "I am Jehovah, the Elohim of Abraham thy father, and the Elohim of Isaac . . ." (Gen. 28:13). It is much easier and more satisfactory to conceive here of a spiritual significance, a divine purpose in a single revelation, and a unity of authorship in the use of these divine names. It is incredible that God should have revealed Himself (as many of these critics have claimed) to one person only as Elohim, and to another person or group only as Jehovah, and then left it to later unknown writers to take bits from here and there and fit them together like a jigsaw puzzle. The wonder and glory of the divine Person in His character and relationships as revealed in His names could hardly have been inspired in such fashion.

DERIVATION AND MEANING OF THE NAME

The name *Jehovah* is derived from the Hebrew verb *havah,* "to be," or "being." This word is almost exactly like the Hebrew verb, *chavah,* "to live," or "life." One can readily see the connection between being and life. Thus when we read the name Jehovah, or Lord in capital letters, in our Bible we think in terms of being or existence and life, and we must think of Jehovah as the Being who is absolutely self-existent, the One who in Himself possesses essential life, permanent existence. It is worth observing in this connection that the Hebrew personal pronoun translated "he" in our Bible is strikingly similar in the Hebrew to the verb *havah,* which means being. And in some significant passages, the word *he,* used of God, is the equivalent to the true and eternal God, that is, the One who always exists, eternal and unchangeable. For instance, we read in Isaiah 43:10, 11: "I am he: before me there was no Elohim formed, neither shall there be after me. I, even I, am Jehovah; and beside me there is no saviour." Then in Psalm 102:27 we read: "But thou art the *same,* and thy years shall have no end." Literally translated, it should read: "Thou art *he,* and thy years shall have no end"; the *he,* so much like the Hebrew word for being, is the equivalent of "the same," the One of old whose years have no end—that is, without beginning and without end.

The most noted Jewish commentator of the Middle Ages, Moses Maimonides, said with regard to this name: "All the names of God which occur in Scripture are derived from His works except one, and that is Jehovah; and this is called the plain name, because it teaches plainly and unequivocally of the substance of God." Another has said: "In the name Jehovah the personality of the Supreme is distinctly expressed. It is everywhere a proper name denoting the person of God, and Him only . . . Elohim . . . denoting usually . . . the Supreme. The Hebrew may say *the* Elohim, the true God, in opposition to all false gods; but he never says *the* Jehovah, for Jehovah is the name of the true God only. He says again and again, my God or my Elohim, but never my *Jehovah,* for when he says my God he means Jehovah. He speaks of the God (*Elohim*) *of Israel* but never of *the Jehovah of Israel,* for there is no other Jehovah. He speaks of *the living God,* but never of *the living Jehovah,* for he cannot conceive of Jehovah as other than living."[1]

RELATION TO ISRAEL

The origin and meaning of the name *Jehovah* are especially brought out in relation to Israel. When Moses at the burning bush says to God: "Behold, when I come

---

[1] Girdlestone, *Old Testament Synonyms,* p. 62.

unto the children of Israel, and shall say unto them,
The Elohim of your fathers hath sent me unto you; and
they shall say unto me, What is his name? what shall I
say unto them?" And the Lord said to Moses, "I am that
I am." The words could be rendered, "I will be that I
will be," and often the word is used in that sense, "I
will be with thee." Its origin is exactly the same as that
of Jehovah—being, existence—and certainly denotes
the One who will always be: personal, continuous, absolute existence.

The point here, however, is that when God wished
to make a special revelation of Himself, He used the
name *Jehovah*. As Jehovah, He is especially the God
of revelation to creatures who can apprehend and appreciate the Infinite—the becoming One. "Thus shalt
thou say unto the children of Israel, I Am hath sent me
unto you . . . Jehovah, the Elohim of your fathers . . .
of Abraham . . . of Isaac, and . . . of Jacob, hath sent
me unto you: this is my name forever, and this is my
memorial unto all generations" (Exod. 3:14, 15). Then
in Exodus 6:2, 3 is written: "I am Jehovah: and I appeared unto Abraham, unto Isaac, and unto Jacob, as
El-Shaddai [God Almighty], and as to my name Jehovah, I was not understood [known] by them; yet verily I
have established my covenant with them, to give them
the land of Canaan."

We have already noted that the name *Jehovah* appears as early as Genesis 2 and certainly it is used with
special significance in regard to God's rational, moral
creatures, but the two passages above do suggest: (1)
that though the name *Jehovah* is thus frequently used
as the title of the Elohim of the Patriarchs, its full significance was not revealed to them; (2) it was now re-

vealed in connection with God's covenant and promise
to a people; (3) that now, after some hundreds of years,
the true significance of the name was to be unfolded by
the manifestation of God as a personal, living Being,
fulfilling to the people of Israel the promises made to
their fathers. Here then, the ever living God reveals
Himself to His covenant people, as the unchanging God
who remains faithful to His word through many generations. "God's personal existence, the continuity of His
dealings with man, the unchangeableness of His promises, and the whole revelation of His redeeming mercy
gathers round the name Jehovah."[2]

Elohim is the general name of God concerned with
the creation and preservation of the world, that is, His
works. As Jehovah, He is the God of revelation in the
expression of Himself in His essential moral and spiritual attributes. But He is especially, as Jehovah, the God
of revelation to Israel. To Japheth and his descendants,
He is the Elohim, the transcendent Deity, but to Shem
and his descendants, through Abraham and Isaac, He is
Jehovah, the God of revelation. All the nations had their
elohim: and even had they retained the true and only
Elohim in their knowledge, He would still have been
to them chiefly Elohim. But the Elohim of Israel (when
they were not backsliding) was Jehovah, who had especially revealed Himself to them. Thus the constant
cry of the faithful Israelite was, "O Jehovah, thou art
our Elohim" (II Chron. 14:11), "Thou art Elohim
alone" (Ps. 86:10).

It is interesting, as one writer points out, to note the
change of these two names of the Deity throughout the

---

[2] *Op. cit.,* p. 64.

Old Testament beyond Exodus 6:3. Such universalistic books as Ecclesiastes, Daniel, Jonah, have Elohim almost exclusively. On the other hand, the strong theocratic and historical books relating to Israel, such as Joshua, Judges, Samuel, Kings, have chiefly Jehovah. The same is true of the Psalms, which may be divided on this basis into two parts. Psalms 42 to 84 almost exclusively use Elohim and other compound names of God; while the other psalms use chiefly Jehovah. It is not merely a matter of difference of authors, for psalms in both sections are ascribed to David. It is rather a difference of purpose.

Thus to Israel, the medium of the revelation of Himself through the Word—the *written Word*—and the medium also of the revelation of Himself in the flesh—the *living Word*—He is especially Jehovah, the God of revelation, the ever-becoming One. Yes, and "the coming One" too, the One who shall be, to appear for man's redemption; the permanent and unchangeable One, for "I am Jehovah; I change not"; "the same yesterday, today and forever." And in this revelation of Himself it is never "thus saith God" or Elohim, but always "thus saith the Lord" or Jehovah.

JEHOVAH—THE GOD OF RIGHTEOUSNESS AND HOLINESS AND LOVE

The name Jehovah has still further significance for us in that it reveals God as a God of moral and spiritual attributes. One could, perhaps, assume that the Elohim, as the mighty omnipotent One who created this vast universe, and who, within the Godhead, covenanted to preserve it, possessed these attributes, but the name and

usage of the title Jehovah clearly reveals it. Whereas
the term Elohim assumes a love toward all creation and
creatures as the work of His hands, the name *Jehovah*
reveals this love as conditioned upon moral and spiritual
attributes. In this connection it is significant that the
name *Jehovah,* as we have already noted, does not
appear till Genesis 2:4. Till then the narrative is concerned only with the general account of the entire creation. But now begins the special account of the creation
of man and God's special relationship to man as distinct
from the lower creation. God now comes into communion with the one whom He has made in His image, and
the Elohim now is called Jehovah-Elohim, who blesses
the earth for the sake of man, His representative upon
it. "The Creator called man into existence as the one
being on earth who should have capacity for the enjoy-
ment of God; and the attributes which appear in the
name 'Jehovah,' and which were not wanted for the creation of material world, were only made visible when
man came forth from God's hand."[3]

It is as Jehovah that God places man under moral
obligations with a warning of punishment for disobedience. Thou shalt and thou shalt not. How significant in
the light of this that when Satan tempts Eve to disobedience he does not mention the name *Jehovah,* but
only *Elohim,* nor does Eve mention it in her reply to
him. Is it because the name *Jehovah* is not known to
them, or rather because deliberate purpose on Satan's
part to deceive and an incipient sense of guilt within
Eve suppress that name? Can one do evil and mention
that name at the same time? And how significant, too,

---

[3] Webb-Peploe, *Titles of Jehovah,* p. 12.

that after their sin they hide, and then hear the voice of
Jehovah-God in the garden, saying, "Where art thou?"
demanding an account of their actions.

That image of Jehovah-God in which man was created is revealed to us in the New Testament as "righteousness and true holiness" (Eph. 4:24). To Israel
of old righteousness and holiness were the two great
attributes associated with the name *Jehovah*. So holy
and sacred was that name to them that they feared to
pronounce it. Perhaps that fear was based on Moses'
injunction that they should not profane that name, and
the penalty of death imposed for blasphemy of the name
Jehovah (Lev. 24:16); but to this day the name *Jehovah* is never read in the synagogue nor uttered by this
people, the word *Adonai* being substituted for it, and by
many simply a word meaning *"the Name."* Thus the
original pronunciation of that name we call Jehovah,
regarded as too sacred to be uttered, has been lost to this
day. Indeed, orthodox Jewry will regard it as a sign of
Messiahship in the one who can truly pronounce it.

Jehovah is righteous, He loveth righteousness (Ps.
11:7); Jehovah our Elohim is righteous in all His
works (Dan. 9:14). "Just and right is he," says Moses.
And "shall not the Judge of all the earth do right," says
Abraham to the Jehovah before whom he stood (Gen.
18:25). The holiness of this Jehovah is magnified
throughout the Old Testament. His first requirement of
those who should be His witnesses is: "Ye shall be holy:
for I Jehovah your Elohim, am holy" (Lev. 19:2).
"Holy, holy, holy is Jehovah of hosts," cry the seraphim,
and that is His glory. Jehovah is ever the Holy One of
Israel.

It is this righteousness of Jehovah against which man

sins. And a righteous Jehovah whose holiness is thus violated and outraged must condemn unrighteousness and punish it. So it is Jehovah who pronounces judgment and metes out punishment. It is Jehovah who sends man forth from the garden, for Jehovah is of purer eyes than to behold evil (Hab. 1:13). Jehovah "created man to enjoy and to exhibit His righteousness." So He demands righteousness and justice and holiness from the creatures made in His image. It is as Jehovah that He looks upon a wicked and corrupt earth and says, "I will destroy." It is as Jehovah that He rains fire and brimstone upon an iniquitous Sodom and Gomorrah. It is as Jehovah that He is angered so often against a sinning, wicked Israel. It is Jehovah who says to Moses: "Whosoever hath sinned against me, him will I blot out of my book" (Exod. 32:33).

But as Jehovah He is also Love. His love makes Him grieve and suffer for the sins and sorrows of His creatures. "I have loved thee with an everlasting love," says Jeremiah (31:3) of Jehovah. In the Book of Judges we read again and again (10:6, 7, etc.) that when Israel forsook Jehovah and served the elohim of the peoples about them, Jehovah's anger brought grievous punishment upon them; but of the same Jehovah it is said: "His soul was grieved for the misery of Israel" (Judges 10:16). "In all their afflictions he was afflicted," says Isaiah (63:9) in a context full of the love and pity of Jehovah. "How can I give thee up O Ephraim . . . my heart heaves within me, my repentings, together they are kindled" (Hosea 11:8).

But while, as Jehovah, His holiness must condemn, He is also Love, and His love redeems; and He seeks to bring man back into fellowship with Himself. So, as one

writer says: "Wherever the name 'Jehovah' appears, after man has fallen from original righteousness, what see
we—but that God is ever seeking the restoration of
man."[1] He comes seeking Adam and Eve. He teaches
man how to approach Him anew by means of sacrifice,
a substitute. This is the clear implication of Abel's approach to God through the sacrifice of a life, and the
rejection of Cain's approach for lack of it. In the whole
sacrificial system, both in the Patriarchal and Levitical
dispensations, the object of approach is Jehovah as distinct from Elohim. It is interesting to note in this connection that in the first seven chapters of Leviticus,
which especially set forth the system of sacrifice, *Elohim* occurs only once alone, and once together with *Jehovah,* while *Jehovah* occurs eighty-six times. The same
is true of the sixteenth chapter of this book which
speaks of the great Day of Atonement, where only the
name *Jehovah* occurs, and that, twelve times. It is further interesting to note in connection with the account
of the Ark and the Flood that in Genesis 6:22 we read
that Noah did according to all that God (Elohim)
commanded him, while in Genesis 7:5 it is said that
Noah did according to all that *Jehovah* commanded
him. The context will reveal that in the first reference
the name *Elohim* is used with reference to the bringing
in of two of every kind of creature into the Ark, for
their preservation. The mighty Elohim who has created
is also the Covenant-Elohim who has covenanted to
preserve that creation. In Genesis 7:5, however, the
name *Jehovah* is used in connection with the command
to bring into the Ark seven pairs of every clean beast.

---

[1] *Op. cit.,* p. 12.

It is not merely for preservation now but for that sacrifice upon which forgiveness and fellowship with Jehovah are based. It was of these clean beasts that Noah offered burnt offerings to Jehovah after the flood.[5]

At the close of the fourth chapter of Genesis, that chapter of tragedy for Adam and Eve, the new son born to them is named Enos, which is a word for man denoting a weak and fallen state. It signifies helplessness. And then men began to call on the name of Jehovah. Weak, helpless man finds he needs more than the mighty, omnipotent, transcendent Being signified by the name *Elohim*. He needs that favor and fellowship with the divine Being for which he was made, and which is signified by *Jehovah*. It is the attribute of love in Jehovah which restores to communion with Himself that man who has sinned against His righteousness and holiness. "From the earliest days the name of Jehovah was taken as the embodiment of that hope for the human race which found expression in sacrifice and in prayer."[6]

So the love in Jehovah does not forsake fallen man. His Spirit continues to strive with man in a period of utter corruption. It is as Jehovah He manifests Himself in covenants and acts of deliverance and redemption. To the children of Israel in cruel and groveling bondage He says, "I am Jehovah, I will bring you out" (Exod. 6:6).

God is always Jehovah to Israel because of His great redemption and deliverance of them. He is in constant communication with Moses. His glory descends upon the tabernacle like a cloud, and Jehovah speaks with Moses face to face as a man speaks to his friend (Exod. 33:9, 11). What a marvelous passage, and how reveal-

---

[5] Jukes, *The Names of God in Holy Scripture,* p. 47.
[6] Girdlestone, *Old Testament Synonyms,* p. 65.

ing of what is contained in that wonderful name in Exodus 34:5-7: "And Jehovah descended in the cloud . . . and proclaimed Jehovah by name. And Jehovah passed by before him, and proclaimed, Jehovah, Jehovah, a God merciful and gracious, slow to anger, and abundant in lovingkindness and truth; keeping lovingkindness for thousands, forgiving iniquity and transgression, and sin" (A.S.V.)!

Speaking of a day of redemption in grace even yet in the future Zechariah says: "I will say it is my people, and they shall say, Jehovah is my God" (Zech. 13:9). Jehovah, yea, even Jehovah is my God. It is Jehovah that Isaiah says is "a just God and a Saviour." "Look unto me and be ye saved all the ends of the earth. . . . Only in Jehovah is righteousness and strength; even to him shall men come" (Isa. 45:22, 24). "Blessed," indeed, "the people who know the joyful sound: O Jehovah in the light of thy countenance they shall walk. In thy name [Jehovah] they shall rejoice all the day: and in thy righteousness they shall be exalted" (Ps. 89:15, 16).

3

EL-SHADDAI

IN OUR DISCUSSION of the name *Jehovah* it was discovered that the first great revelation of the significance of that name was given to Israel in Egypt. They were the people of His covenant with Abraham, and Isaac, and Jacob, a separated people through whom a righteous and holy God would work out His purpose of redemption for mankind. In Exodus 3:14, 15, He thus revealed Himself: "I am that I am . . . Thus shalt thou say unto the children of Israel, Jehovah, the God of your fathers, the God of Abraham, the God of Isaac, and the God of Jacob, hath sent me unto you: this is my name forever and ever, and this is my memorial unto all generations." Then in Exodus 6:2, 3 it is written: "And God spake unto Moses, and said unto him, I am Jehovah: and I appeared unto Abraham, unto Isaac, and unto Jacob, as God Almighty, but by my name Jehovah, I was not known [or was not made known] to them." It was suggested that by this it was meant that the Patriarchs had not understood the full significance of that name. Naturally the full significance of a name which means the ever-existent One, the eternal, the *ever-becoming One*—that is, the One continually revealing Himself and His ways and purposes could not be under-

stood except after centuries and centuries of unfolding
of events and experiences. The point here is, however,
that God was known especially to the Patriarchs by this
name *God Almighty,* or in the Hebrew, *El-Shaddai.*

The name appears first in connection with Abraham.
In Genesis 17:1, 2, we read, "And when Abram was
ninety years old and nine, Jehovah appeared to Abram,
and said unto him, I am *God Almighty* [El-Shaddai];
walk before me, and be thou perfect. And I will make
my covenant between me and thee, and will multiply
thee exceedingly." The occasion was the confirmation
of a promise already made to Abram to make him a
great nation (Gen. 12:2), to make his seed as the dust
of the earth innumerable (Gen. 13:16), and (Gen.
15:5), like the stars of heaven, referring perhaps to a
spiritual seed, also innumerable. Then we are told that
Abram believed Jehovah, who reckoned it to him for
righteousness. But the years passed, and Abram had
no child. He was getting to be an old man and Sarai an
old woman. Still there was no seed. That faith which
God had reckoned to him for righteousness was beginning to dim a little. Then it lapsed for a while, and
they adopted that fleshly and unfortunate expedient
which brought Ishmael and Mohammedanism into the
world, but did not bring the fulfillment of the promise.
Again the years went by and Abraham was ninety-nine
years old, and the promise, by human reckoning, was
now impossible of fulfillment. But is anything too hard
for Jehovah? Nothing is impossible with Him! And it is
precisely at this point and in this connection, as we shall
see later, that the promise of a seed is confirmed, and
the name of Abram changed to Abraham with the revelation of God as El-Shaddai, or God Almighty.

Derivation and Meaning of the Name

Now what does the term *God Almighty* mean? We might begin by saying what it does not mean, and by ridding ourselves of a common misconception. True, the word *almighty* does suggest the all-powerful, the mighty, the power to be able to do anything and everything at any time. Certainly there cannot be anything beyond God's power. But this is indicated in the word *God* in this name, and not so much in the word we translate "almighty." The word for God here is *El*—El-Shaddai— God Almighty. In our first study, we discovered that the name *Elohim* is derived primarily from this word *el,* and that it stood for might, power, omnipotence, transcendence, the name connected especially with Creation. We learned that the word *el* itself is translated "God" over 200 times in the Bible with that general significance. "Thou art the El that doest wonders: thou hast made known thy strength among the peoples" (Ps. 77:14). He is "the El of Israel who giveth strength and might to the people" (Ps. 68:35). And Moses says of Him: "What El is there in the heavens or in the earth who can do according to thy works, and according to thy might?" (Deut. 3:24). It is the word Isaiah uses in the wonderful fortieth chapter of his prophecy of the mighty, incomparable God. It is the word often used to denote God's power to interpose or intervene. So Nehemiah calls upon the great, the mighty, and the terrible El to intervene in behalf of His people (9:32).

This word *el* is also translated by such words as "might" and "power," with regard to men. Laban says to Jacob: "It is in the power of my hand to do you hurt" (Gen. 31:29). The word for power is *el*. In Proverbs

3:27 we read: "Withhold not good from them to whom it is due, when it is in the power [the el] of thine hand to do it." "They practice evil," says Micah (2:1), "because it is in the power of their hand." The psalmist speaks of Him as "the *El* that girdeth me with strength" (18:32).

It seems clear, then, with regard to this name *God Almighty,* or *El-Shaddai,* that the idea of all might and all power is abundantly expressed in the term *God* or *El.* How, then, shall we understand that part of the name called Almighty or Shaddai?

In the first place, it is true that there is some difference of opinion as to the root meaning of this word. The translation of it as "almighty" is due to the influence of that ancient Latin version of the Bible called the Vulgate, which dates back to the fourth century A.D., and was written by Jerome. There are some scholars who simply dismiss the matter by saying its derivation is doubtful. Other modern scholars believe it comes from a root meaning strong, powerful, or to do violence, especially in the sense of one who is so powerful as to be able to set aside or do violence to the laws of nature or the ordinary course of nature. It is true that this is what happened in connection with the revelation of this name to Abraham, for the deadness of their bodies was overcome, and Isaac was born in fulfillment of the promise after their bodies were considered dead. Thus one scholar writes that "Elohim is the God who creates nature so that it is and supports it so that it continues, El-Shaddai the God who compels nature to do what is contrary to itself." And so another says that as El-Shaddai He reveals Himself by special deeds of power.

It is quite likely that there is some connection between

the name *Shaddai* and the root from which some modern scholars think it is derived, but in view of the circumstances under which it is often used and in view of the translation of another word almost exactly like it, we believe it has another derivation and a more significant meaning than that of special power.

Shaddai itself occurs forty-eight times in the Old Testament and is translated "almighty." The other word so like it, and from which we believe it to be derived, occurs twenty-four times and is translated "breast." As connected with the word *breast,* the title *Shaddai* signifies one who nourishes, supplies, satisfies. Connected with the word for God, *El,* it then becomes the "One mighty to nourish, satisfy, supply." Naturally with God the idea would be intensified, and it comes to mean the One who "sheds forth" and "pours" out sustenance and blessing. In this sense, then, God is the all-sufficient, the all-bountiful. For example, Jacob upon his death-bed, blessing his sons and forecasting their future, says in Genesis 49:24, 25, concerning Joseph: ". . . the arms of his hands were made strong by the hands of the mighty God of Jacob . . . even by the God [El] of thy father, who shall help thee; and by the *Almighty* [*Shaddai*], who shall bless thee with blessings of heaven above, blessings of the deep that lieth under, blessings of the breasts and of the womb." The distinction and significance of names here is quite striking and obvious. It is God as El who helps, but it is God as Shaddai who abundantly blesses with all manner of blessings, and blessings of the breast.

This derivation as related to God is even more strikingly brought out in two passages in the Book of Isaiah. In 60:15, 16, speaking of the restoration of the people

Israel in the future, Isaiah says: "Whereas thou hast been forsaken and hated . . . I will make thee an eternal excellency, a joy of many generations. Thou shalt also suck the milk of the nations, and shalt suck the breast of kings: and [thus] thou shalt know that I Jehovah am thy Saviour and thy Redeemer, the mighty One of Jacob." Here the idea of bounty under the figure of blessings of the breast is directly associated with God. In Isaiah 66:10-13, one of the most beautiful passages of Scripture, it is even more directly expressed. In verses 10 and 11 the prophet calls upon all who love Jerusalem and mourn over her to rejoice and be glad in her redemption and restoration. "That ye may suck and be satisfied with the breasts of her consolations; that ye may milk out, and be delighted with the abundance of her glory." In verse 12 he continues: "For thus saith Jehovah, Behold, I will extend peace to her like a river, and the glory of the nations like a flowing stream: then shall ye suck. . . ." and in verse 13: "as one whom his mother comforteth, so will I comfort you; and ye shall be comforted in Jerusalem." The point is that the word translated "breast" in these passages is the Hebrew *shad* from which is derived *Shaddai,* the name of God translated "almighty" in our Bibles.

In that ancient version of the Bible we call the Septuagint, translated by Jewish scholars from the Hebrew into Greek more than 250 years B.C., this name *Shaddai* is rendered a number of times by a Greek word *ikanos* which can be translated "all-sufficient." The ancient rabbis also said that the word *shaddai* was made up of two particles which, put together, meant "sufficient" or "self-sufficient."

Such a conception of a god or deity was not uncommon to the ancients. The idols of the ancient heathen are sometimes termed *sheddim* in the Bible. It is no doubt because they were regarded as the great agents of nature or the heavens, in giving rain, in causing the earth to send forth its springs, to yield its increase, its fruits to maintain and to nourish life. There were many-breasted idols worshiped among the heathen. One historian points out that "the whole body of the Egyptian goddess Isis was clustered over with breasts because all things are sustained or nourished by the earth or nature." The same was true of the idol of the Ephesian goddess Diana in Acts 19, for Diana signified nature and the world with all its products. Ancient inscriptions on some of these idols of Diana read: "All-various nature, mother of all things."[1] It is interesting to observe here that the common Hebrew word for field (*sadeh*)—that is, a cultivated field—is simply another form of the word *shaddai*. It is the field as cultivated earth which nourishes and sustains life.

Thus in this name God is seen to be the power or shedder-forth of blessings, the all-sufficient and the all-bountiful One. Of course, the idea of One who is all powerful and all mighty is implied in this; for only an all-powerful One could be all sufficient and all bountiful. He is almighty because He is able to carry out His purposes and plans to their fullest and most glorious and triumphant completion. He is able to triumph over every obstacle and over all opposition; that is, He is sufficient for all these things. He is able, we are told, to subdue all things to Himself. But the word *able* applied to God refers more than anything else to what He wants

---

[1] Parkhurst, *Hebrew Lexicon* (*see* Sheddim).

to be and to do for man. So He is able to save to the uttermost. And He is able to do exceedingly abundantly above all that we can ask or think. From all this it is felt that the name *El-Shaddai* or *God Almighty* is much better understood as that El who is all sufficient and all bountiful, the source of all blessing and fullness and fruitfulness. This leads us to our next consideration.

THE USE AND SIGNIFICANCE OF THE NAME

Let us look again for a moment at the circumstances under which this name was first revealed. To a man who apparently had some measure of understanding about the one true God and who gave some promise of faith; who left a settled and assured abode, comfortable circumstances, and family and friends to go on a long hazardous journey he knew not whither, God made certain promises: the promise of a land, a large posterity, and a spiritual mission. He was fairly well advanced in years when the promise was first made. For many years his faith stood the test of waiting while God repeatedly assured him of the promise. When it appeared, however, that soon it would be too late, humanly speaking, for such a promise to be fulfilled, he took matters into his own hands, and Ishmael was born of Hagar, of the will of man, of the will of the flesh and not of God.

God allowed thirteen years more to pass, till it was no longer possible according to the flesh that the child of promise should be born. Then when God appears to him again to repeat the promise of a seed Abraham can only think in terms of Ishmael and begs that he might be allowed to live and the promise made sure in him. Yet he laughs with a mixture of both doubt and hope within that it may yet be true. Perhaps faith predominates as he says in heart: "Shall a child be born to him that is a hundred years old? And shall Sarah that is ninety years old, bear?" (Gen. 17:17). It was to this faith in God's promise that Paul refers in Romans 4:19-21 that Abraham "staggered not at the promise of God," and did not consider his own body as good as dead or Sarah's, and was fully persuaded that what God promised He was able to perform. And the Epistle to the Hebrews refers to Sarah's faith, who received strength to give birth when past age (11:11). It is then that God reveals Himself to Abraham as El-Shaddai, mighty in sufficiency and dispensing of His bounty. He is, first of all, sufficient to revive the deadness of the human body in order to show His great power and bounty.

It was a staggering promise by the time it was finally repeated, but they did not stagger at it. It is by this new name, in this connection, that God now reveals Himself as the Mighty Promiser and Giver of gifts. Abraham and Sarah had to learn that what God promises only God can give, that the promise was not to be made sure by the works of the flesh. So the bodies of both of them must die first to make them realize that it was all of God. Jacob had to be made lame and halt before he could finally reenter the land of promise, lest he should claim it as acquired by his own hand and cunning, and boast of his own sufficiency. So, too, God's salvation in Christ is His gift to us and not to be earned by anything we may do—"not of works lest any man should boast."

Thus this name also taught Abraham his own insufficiency, the futility of relying upon his own efforts and the folly of impatiently running ahead of God. Numberless Christian people have been guilty of just this, often to their sorrow and loss. The birth of Ishmael proved to be a sore trial, not only in Abraham's household, but to Abraham's descendants, both physical and spiritual, all through the ages. God as El-Shaddai is sufficient for all things. Man's meddling only mars His working. It is significant that with the revelation of this name Abraham is enjoined to "walk before me, and be thou perfect." Instead of *perfect,* the word *complete* or *wholehearted* would much better express what is meant. The point is that Abraham's faith had been marred by the fleshly and self-sufficient expedient to which he had resorted. The mighty all-sufficient One demands and deserves our complete faith—a wholehearted faith.

Then this name introduces God to us as the all-bountiful in the fullness and fruitfulness He imparts to all who trust Him and wait patiently upon Him. This is most clearly set forth and illustrated in the first few occasions of the use of this name. As God Almighty or El-Shaddai, God changes the name *Abram,* which means "exalted father," to *Abraham,* which means "father of a multitude," many nations. "I will make thee exceeding fruitful, and I will make nations of thee, and kings shall come out of thee" (Gen. 17:6). In blessing Jacob, Isaac says (Gen. 28:3): "El-Shaddai bless thee, and make thee fruitful, and multiply thee, that thou mayest be a multitude of people." In Genesis 35:11, God Himself says to Jacob: "I am El-Shaddai: be fruitful and multiply; a nation and a company of nations shall be of thee, and kings shall come out of thy loins." Jacob upon his deathbed re-

peats the promise of a great posterity made in the
name of El-Shaddai (Gen. 48:3, 4), and in that name
pronounces the same blessing upon Joseph, the blessings of Heaven and earth and of the breasts and of
the womb (Gen. 49:25).

It is the name used by Balaam, who, being hired to
curse Israel, was compelled to turn it into a blessing.
It is the "vision of the Almighty" (Num. 24:4, 16)
which makes him see Israel a goodly people, spread
out, with its seed in many waters, and as final victor
over all its enemies through that Star of Jacob and
the Scepter of Israel, its Messiah. Certainly this significance of the name may be gathered from the Book
of Job, where it occurs thirty-one out of the forty-
eight times it appears in the Old Testament, for the
end of Job was even more blessed and abundantly
fruitful than his beginning.

It is in this connection that another aspect of the
name *El-Shaddai*, as the One who fills and makes fruitful, appears. We have already seen that to experience
God's sufficiency one must realize one's own insufficiency. To experience God's fullness one must empty
self. It is not easy to empty self. It was never easy to
do that. The less empty of self we are, the less of blessing God can pour into us; the more of pride and self-
sufficiency, the less fruit we can bear. Sometimes only
chastening can make us realize this. Thus it is that the
name *Almighty God* or *El-Shaddai* is used in connection with judging, chastening, purging. Is it not significant that it is in connection with the loss of her home,
her husband and her two sons, the fruit of her womb,
that Naomi says: "The Almighty [Shaddai] hath dealt
very bitterly with me"? "I went out full, and the Lord

hath brought me home again empty . . . the Almighty
[again Shaddai] hath afflicted me" (Ruth 1:20, 21).
And as in the case of Naomi is it not also true of Job
that even this "perfect and upright" man was made
more upright or whole through sufferings; that he was
purged, through chastening, of some imperfections
which hindered his fullest blessing and fruitfulness;
that this chastening emptied him so completely of self
that he could be "filled with all the fullness of God"?
(Eph. 3:19). He understood this in the day when he
said: "But now mine eye seeth thee. Wherefore I abhor
myself, and repent in dust and ashes" (Job 42:5, 6).
Then he received power with God to intercede for his
friends, and he was filled with double blessings.

The same El-Shaddai of the Old Testament is the
One who in the New chastens whom He loves that,
being exercised thereby, they may yield the peaceable
fruit of holiness or righteousness. He is the same One
who has chosen us to bring forth fruit, much fruit, and
that this fruit should remain (John 15:16). As the all-
sufficient One He says, "Without me ye can do nothing"
(John 15:5). As the all-abounding One who makes us
fruitful with His gifts, He finds it necessary to purge us
that we may bring forth more fruit (John 15:2).

In the Book of Revelation the name *Almighty* appears in connection with the pouring out of judgments.
Of the Lord God Almighty it is said, "True and righteous are thy judgments" (16:7). We read of "the war
of the great day of God, the Almighty" (16:14), and
19:15 speaks of "the fierceness of the wrath of God
the Almighty." May it not be that this is simply the
opposite aspect of that name which signifies the pouring forth of blessings! Of the new heavens and new

earth in chapter 21 we are told that the Lord God Almighty and the Lamb are its temple (v. 22), and its glory and light (v. 23). But the Lamb which was the last word and full manifestation of God's outpouring of love and life upon man is the Lamb slain—rejected and slain of man. It is from the wrath of the Lamb that men hide. It is the Lamb, too, who opens the seals and pours out judgment. If man will not receive fullness of love and life from God, he must receive judgment. For He who poured out His blood that men might have life and have it more abundantly must pour out the judgment of sin and death upon all who will not receive it.

But even here the ultimate purpose is of love and mercy. The judgment of some is to turn to the mercy of many, that He may see of the travail of His soul and be satisfied, that ten thousand times ten thousand may gather about the throne and sing the song of the all-bountiful, all-merciful God and of the Lamb.

So we see that the name *Almighty God* speaks to us of the inexhaustible stores of His bounty, of the riches and fulness of His grace in self-sacrificing love pouring itself out for others. It tells us that from God comes every good and perfect gift, that He never wearies of pouring His mercies and blessings upon His people. But we must not forget that His strength is made perfect in our weakness; His sufficiency is most manifest in our insufficiency; His fullness in our emptiness, that being filled, from us may flow rivers of living water to a thirsty and needy humanity.

4

ADONAI

THE NAMES OF GOD we have studied so far have been *Elohim,* translated "God" in our Bibles; *Jehovah,* translated "LORD"; and *"El-Shaddai,"* translated "God Almighty" or "Almighty God." These names have related rather to the Person of God—the power and glory of His Being, as in Elohim; the expression of Himself as a God of righteousness, holiness, love and redemption, as in Jehovah; and as a beneficent and bountiful Bestower of powers, gifts, blessings, and fruitfulness for service, as seen in El-Shaddai. While these names do imply or demand a responsibility on the part of man to conform to the Being in whose image he is made, the name under consideration in this chapter makes a definite claim upon man's obedience and service.

The name *Adonai* is translated in our Bibles by the word *Lord* in small letters, only the first of which is a capital. Used as a name of God, *Adonai* occurs probably some 300 times in the Old Testament. It is significant that it is almost always in the plural and possessive, meaning my Lords'. It confirms the idea of a trinity as found also in the name *Elohim.* This is still further confirmed by the fact that the same word is used of men some 215 times and translated variously "master," "sir," and "lord," but for the most part, "master," as throughout Genesis 24, where Eliezer, the servant of Abraham, speaks of "my master Abraham," and over and over again says, "Blessed be Jehovah God of my master Abraham." It is important to notice, too, that the same word *Adonai* is translated a number of times by the word "owner." But, used of men, it is always in the singular form, *adon*. Only of God is it in the plural. The suggestion of the Trinity in this name is still more strikingly confirmed by its use in Psalm 110, in these words: "The Lord said unto my Lord," or "Jehovah said unto my Adonai. Sit thou on my right hand, till I make thine enemies thy footstool." The Lord Jesus in Matthew 22:41-45 (as also Peter, Acts 2:34, 35; and Hebrews 1:13; 10:12, 13) refers this striking passage to Himself. How significant then that David, speaking of but one member of the Trinity, should use here not the plural *Adonai,* but the singular form *Adoni:* "Jehovah said unto my Adoni," that is to Christ, the second Person of the Trinity!

The name *Adonai,* while translated "Lord," signifies ownership or mastership and indicates "the truth that God is the owner of each member of the human family, and that He consequently claims the unrestricted obedience of all."[1] The expression, "Lord of lords," in Deuteronomy 10:17, could be rendered "Master of masters." An illustration of this name as a claim upon man's obedience and service is found in Malachi 1:6: "A son honoreth his father, and a servant his master: if then I be a father, where is mine

---

[1] Girdlestone, *Old Testament Synonyms,* p. 59.

honor? And if I be a master, where is my fear? saith
Jehovah of hosts . . ." And in Job 28:28 it is declared
that the fear of Adonai (the Lord, the Master) is wisdom.

THE USE OF THE WORD IN THE OLD TESTAMENT

The use of this name *Adonai* in the Old Testament
plainly reveals the relationship which God sustains toward His creatures and what He expects of them. A
glance at a good concordance will give all the instances in which the name occurs. Let us examine a
few of them.

The first occasion of its use, as with the name *El-
Shaddai,* is with Abraham in Genesis 15:2. In the first
verse of this chapter it is written: "After these things"
—that is, after his rescue of Lot and his military
achievement of the defeat of the four kings and their
armies, where it is revealed that Abraham himself was
lord or master (adon) of a large establishment—"After these things the word of Jehovah came unto Abram
in a vision, saying, Fear not, Abram: I am thy shield,
and thy exceeding great reward." Abram then makes
his reply addressing God as Adonai-Jehovah—an acknowledgment that Jehovah is also Master. Certainly
Abram understood what this relationship meant; perhaps better than we nowadays understand it, for those
were days of slavery. Lordship meant complete possession on the one hand, and complete submission on
the other. As already seen, Abraham himself sustained
the relationship of master and lord over a very con-
siderable number of souls; therefore in addressing Jehovah as Adonai he acknowledged God's complete

possession of and perfect right to all that he was and
had.

But even Abraham, thousands of years ago, understood by this more than mere ownership, more than
the expression and imposition of an arbitrary or capricious will. Even in those days the relationship of master and slave was not altogether or necessarily an un-
mitigated evil. The purchased slave stood in a much
nearer relationship to his lord than the hired servant.
who was free to come and go as he might wish. In
Israel, the hired servant who was a stranger might not
eat of the Passover or the holy things of the master's
house, but the purchased slave, as belonging to his
master, and so a member of the family, possessed this
privilege (Exod. 12:43-45; Lev. 22:10, 11). The slave
had the right of the master's protection and help and
direction. Nor was the relationship devoid of affection.
In the absence of seed, a slave, Eliezer, is the heir to
Abram's entire household. So the psalmist well puts
it all when he says: "Behold, as the eyes of servants
look unto the hand of their masters, and as the eyes of
a maiden unto the hand of her mistress; so our eyes
wait upon the Lord our God . . ." (123:2). "The eyes
of all wait upon thee; and thou givest them their meat
in due season" (Ps. 145:15). As Adonai, or Master
or Lord, God says to Abraham: "Fear not, Abram; I
am thy shield and thy exceeding great reward." He can
depend upon the faithfulness of the Master. For if a
human master can sustain relationships even of affection to a slave and be faithful in provision and protection, how much more the Jehovah-God who is Adonai also to His creatures.

There are many examples of the use of this name

which well illustrate this truth: Moses, when commissioned to go to Egypt to deliver Israel, addresses God as Adonai, acknowledging thus God's right to his life and service when he replies: "O my Lord" (that is, Adonai), "I am not eloquent . . . I am slow of speech" (Exod. 4:10). And again he says after God's reply, "O my Lord [Adonai] send someone else." Then God's anger kindled against him, against a servant who seeks to evade his responsibility of carrying out the will of his rightful Lord. For God, who is never a capricious or unjust Master, does not ask what cannot be performed, and never requires a task for which He does not equip His servants. Thus He assures Moses that He will be his sufficiency for the task (Exod. 4:10).

As the eye of a servant looks to the master, so Joshua, in defeat and distress, looks for direction to the Lord God who is his Adonai. When Gideon is called to deliver the children of Israel from the Midianites, he asks: "O my Lord [Adonai], wherewith shall I save Israel? Behold my family is poor in Manasseh, and I am the least in my father's house" (Judges 6:15). Then God gives answer: "Surely I will be with thee, and thou shalt smite the Midianites as one man." The name *Adonai* is found frequently on the lips of David, and in one especially significant passage in this connection (II Sam. 7:18-20), it appears four times in three verses. To David, of humble origin, a shepherd lad, and now king of Israel, God comes and promises to establish his dynasty, his throne, forever. Overcome by this great promise, for he recognizes in it also the promise of Messiah who shall come from his loins, David, king and lord of God's people, calls God his Lord, coupling it with the name *Jehovah*. He acknowledges his humble origin, his own unworthiness, and the goodness and greatness of God the Adonai who has exalted him, and he says: "Who am I, O Adonai Jehovah? And what is my house, that thou hast brought me hitherto? . . . And what can David say more unto thee? For thou, *Adonai Jehovah*, knowest thy servant."

The psalmists, too, make frequent use of the name in its proper significance. It is Jehovah, Adonai, whose name is so excellent in all the earth, who has put all things under His feet (Ps. 8). He is the Adonai of the whole earth (Ps. 97:5). The earth is bidden to tremble at the presence of the Adonai, its Lord (Ps. 114:7). Adonai is above all elohim or gods (Ps. 135:5). As Master or Lord, Adonai is besought to remember the reproach of His servant (Ps. 89:50). "My eyes are unto thee, O God, the Adonai" (Ps. 141:8) says the psalmist as of a servant to his Lord. And he asks Adonai, his Master, to take up his cause and defend him against his enemies (Ps. 109:21-28).

The use of this name by Isaiah the prophet is especially significant. It is the vision of God as Adonai which started him out on his prophetical career. One of the most stirring portions of Scripture describes this vision. It was a time of national darkness, for Uzziah, Judah's great king, had died. Uzziah was the prophet's king, therefore his lord and master, and perhaps his hero too, in spite of his tragic end. It is then that the young man experiences one of the most solemn and significant visions of Scripture. In the sixth chapter he tells us, "In the year that King Uzziah died I saw the Lord"—Adonai. His earthly lord and master had died, but what does that matter when the Lord of lords, the Adonai in the heavens, lives and reigns. This Adonai is seated upon a throne too, but high and lifted up, above all earthly lords and monarchs, for this Adonai is also Jehovah of hosts, whose train fills the Temple and whose glory covers the whole earth. This Adonai is surrounded by the fiery seraphim, who not only cover their eyes before their thrice holy Lord, but with their wings are ready instantly to do His bidding. Then after the prophet's confession and cleansing in preparation for his service, he hears a voice saying: "Whom shall I send and who will go for us?" This call for service comes from Adonai, for this is the name used in verse 8.

So prophet after prophet is called and commissioned for service by Adonai, the Lord who claims obedience and service. The shrinking Jeremiah, ordained from before his birth to be a prophet, answers the call to service by saying, somewhat like Moses: "Ah, Adonai Jehovah! Behold, I cannot speak: for I am a child" (Jer. 1:6). As with Moses, the Lord of life and service enables His servants to carry out His commands when they yield themselves to Him and obey. He touches the lips of Jeremiah, as of Isaiah, and promises His presence and protection.

In the prophecy of Ezekiel the name *Adonai Jehovah* occurs some 200 times. It has added significance here in that the name occurs in connection with prophecies not only concerning Israel but concerning the nations round about. It reveals that Adonai claims lordship not only over Israel but, whether they will or not, over all the peoples of the earth. It is, "Thus saith Jehovah who is Adonai," and again and again, "Ye shall know," and "They shall know that I am Adonai Jehovah" (Ezek. 13:9; 23:49; 24:24; 28:24; 29:16).

It is Adonai Jehovah who commands the four winds to breathe upon the dry bones and make them live (Ezek. 37:9).

The use of this name is especially notable in Daniel 9 where it occurs ten times in seventeen verses. Daniel is living in the land of Israel's captivity, whose king is lord or adon over many nations; but only Jehovah is the Adonai of Daniel and his people. This is a chapter of confession of Israel's faithlessness as God's servant, hence Daniel addresses God as Adonai in his prayer for forgiveness and restoration of the people and Jerusalem. "O Adonai," he cries, "the great and dreadful God, keeping the covenant and mercy to them that love him, and to them that keep his commandments; we have sinned, and have committed iniquity, and have done wickedly, and have rebelled, even by departing from thy precepts and from thy judgments" (9:4, 5). Since it is God as Lord and Master whose will they have disobeyed, it is He to whom they must address their prayer for forgiveness, for acceptance, for restoration. Thus it is in verse 19, "O Adonai, hear; O Adonai, forgive; O Adonai, hearken and do; defer not, for thine own sake, O my God . . ."

So throughout the Old Testament those who know God as Adonai acknowledge themselves as servants: Abraham, Isaac and Jacob are thus spoken of (Exod. 32:13). Over and over again we read, "Moses, my servant," and "Moses, the servant of the Lord." In the same significant passage in which he addresses God as Adonai, a number of times David the king speaks of himself as "thy servant." "I am thy servant; give me understanding," says the psalmist (Ps. 119:125). The word translated servant is also slave. Thus prophets, priests, kings, all God's people acknowledged themselves His servants, recognizing His right to command and dispose of them according to His will as the Lord of their lives. It is this which is suggested by the name *Lord* or *Adonai*.

ITS USE IN THE NEW TESTAMENT

The meaning of *Adonai* as Lord and Master is carried over into the New Testament. Between two and three centuries before Christ the Hebrew Scriptures were translated into Greek by a group of Jewish translators at Alexandria in Egypt. It is interesting to note that they translated the word *Adonai* in Genesis 15:2 as "Master." In the Greek it is "Despot."

In the New Testament, too, it is the word used of men as lord and master in relationship to servants. It is used hundreds of times of the Lord Jesus Himself.

We are said to be not our own; we have been bought with a price. We belong to God who is our Lord and Master. We are therefore bidden to glorify God in body and spirit, which are His (I Cor. 6:19, 20). Many Scriptures set forth this relationship to God as His servants. We are exhorted to present our bodies as a living sacrifice to God, holy, and acceptable, and this as our reasonable service (Rom. 12:1). We are to understand what is the will of the Lord—our Adonai (Eph. 5:17). And Peter calls us children of obedience to Him who has called us (I Peter 1:14, 15); and He is the Master who has bought us (II Peter 2:1).

A striking illustration of this is found in the life of the apostle Paul. He felt himself to be a zealous servant of the *Lord* God of his fathers even in his first opposition to and persecution of the Church, believing he was doing God great service. The first words that fall from his lips on his conversion are: "Lord [Master], what wilt thou have me to do?" (Acts 9:6). Like a good servant, he tells us that when it pleased God to reveal His Son in him that he might preach Him among the nations, "immediately he conferred not with flesh and blood," but he went away in complete surrender to be alone with his Lord to prepare himself as quickly as possible to do His will (Gal. 1:16, 17). He seems to take even a little pride in emphasizing the Lordship of Jesus Christ by calling himself His bond-servant or slave. As such he bore in his body the marks of his Lord Jesus (Gal. 6:17). "Christ Jesus, my Lord [my Master, my Adonai], counted me faithful, appointing me to his service" (I Tim. 1:12). "I count not my life dear to myself so that I may accomplish my course, and the ministry which I received from the *Lord* Jesus" (Acts 20:24). Whether we live or die, we are the *Lord's* (the Master's).

As in the Old Testament, so in the New, God as Lord is represented as the One who bestows gifts upon and equips His servants for their service. He made some apostles, others prophets, evangelists, pastors, teachers—all for the accomplishment of His purpose and will in the perfecting of the saints, the work of the ministry, and the edifying of the Body of Christ (Eph. 4:11, 12). Having these gifts from our Lord, Paul exhorts us, let us wait on them and minister them, as faithful servants, with diligence (Rom. 12:6-8). God, as Lord, is said to protect, to provide for and sustain His servants. In the Old Testament, Adonai says to Abram, "I am thy shield." He is a rock, a fortress, a deliverer. Luke says of Paul, in great danger: "The Lord stood by him and said, Be of good cheer" (Acts 23:11). Again: "The Lord stood with me and strengthened me" (II Tim. 4:17). The Lord delivers His servants from every evil (II Tim. 4:18). The grace of the Lord is continually with His servants. It is the Lord who says to Paul, "My grace is sufficient for thee" (II Cor. 12:9). The Lord directs the service of His servants, opening doors (II Cor. 2:12), and closing them, too (Acts 16:6). We are exhorted to abound in the work of the Lord for such work is never in vain (I Cor. 15:58).

God's requirements of service and usefulness are clearly set forth in the parables of the Lord Jesus, especially in the parable of the talents (Matt. 25:14-30), and the parable of the pounds (Luke 19:11-27). As Lord, He rewards the faithfulness of His servants and punishes their lack of it. The reward is far more than commensurate with the service rendered. In the parables, the reward is represented in terms of the material, but the real reward is in the realm of the spiritual, of which the material is only a feeble analogy. Even so, the greatness of our reward for faithfulness as servants lies in our increasing apprehension and possession of our Lord Himself. Adonai said to Abram, "I am thy exceeding great reward." Frequently in the Old Testament the Lord is said to be the inheritance, the portion and possession of His people (Num. 18:20; Ps. 73:26; 16:5; Ezek. 44:27, 28). So Christ our Lord gave Himself for us and to us. If we are His, He is ours, and He is ours in proportion as we are His.

Apart from this, however, there is a day of reckoning for His servants. In the Old Testament, Adonai renders to every man according to his work (Ps. 62:12). Every servant's work is to be made manifest. The test of fire will prove its worth. If it stands the test, it will receive a reward. If not, it will be lost (I Cor. 3:13-15). "To whomsoever much is given, of him shall much be required: and to whom they commit much, of him will they ask the more" (Luke 12:48, A.S.V.) "It is required in stewards, that a man be found faithful" (I Cor. 4:2, A.S.V.).

But since God is Lord of all men whether they acknowledge Him or not, there is a day of reckoning for all men apart from His servants. Jeremiah calls it the day of Adonai, Jehovah of hosts (46:10). It is a day of vengeance, for Adonai the Lord will demand a reckoning from all His creatures. But, thank God that the Lord Jesus Christ will be deliverance and surety in that day for all who have believed on and served Him.

It is the Lord Jesus Christ, however, who, though He is our Lord and Master, is the supreme example of the true and faithful servant. He is the ideal servant. It is in Him we realize the full import and blessedness of the relationship that exists between ourselves and God as servant to a Lord. He is revealed in the Old Testament as the Servant. "Behold my servant, whom I uphold; mine elect, in whom my soul delighteth; I have put my spirit upon him" (Isa. 42:1). "He shall not fail" (v. 4). "I the Lord . . . will hold thine hand, and will keep thee . . ." (v. 6). So the New Testament tells us He took the form of a servant—the same word Paul uses of himself, a bondservant, a slave. He humbled Himself and became obedient unto death (Phil. 2:7, 8). "Lo, I come (in the volume of the book it is written of me,) to do thy will, O God" (Heb. 10:7). This is in fulfillment of Psalm 40:6-8 where He is spoken of as the slave whose ear is bored, because he loves his master and elects to serve him forever (Exod. 21:6). He said of Himself, "I do always those things that please him" (John 8:29). "Even Christ pleased not himself," says Paul (Rom. 15:3). "The Son of man came not to be ministered unto, but to minister, and to give his life a ransom for many" (Matt. 20:28). "I am among you as he that serveth" (Luke 22:27). As a servant He also suffered, being made perfect through sufferings (Heb. 2:10). In that wonderful thirteenth chapter of John, He sets Himself forth as our Example as a servant. "Ye call me Master and Lord: and ye say well, for so I am" (v. 13). "I have given you an example, that ye should do as I have done to you. Verily, verily, I say unto you, The servant is not greater than his lord . . ." (vv. 15, 16). He exhorted to faithful service to the end, and spoke of the blessedness of those servants whom the Lord when He comes will find faithful and watching (Luke 12:36, 37).

To be servant of the Lord is the greatest liberty and joy of all. Man needs lordship. With faculties and judgments impaired, distorted by sin, original and personal, he needs direction, guidance, authority in this world. Man is born to worship and serve. If he does not serve God, then directly or indirectly he serves the Devil, the usurper of authority. But no man, as our Lord said, can serve two masters—that is, God and the Devil— at the same time. "Know ye not," says Paul, "that to whom ye yield yourselves servants to obey, his servants ye are to whom ye obey; whether of sin unto death, or of obedience unto righteousness?" (Rom. 6:16). To be subject to Satan is to be abject. His lordship makes service servile. He has made service degraded and a badge of inferiority. Christ, our Lord, Himself the ideal servant, has invested service with dignity, nobility, liberty, joy. "For he that is called in the Lord, being a servant, is the Lord's freeman" (I Cor. 7:22). To be the servant of God is eternal life (Rom. 6:22). And the faithful servant of the Lord will one day hear those joyful words from the lips of the Lord: "Well done, good and faithful servant . . . enter thou into the joy of thy Lord."

5

JEHOVAH-JIREH

THE NAME *Jehovah-jireh* is one of a number of names compounded with Jehovah. Naturally these names owe something of their significance to the name *Jehovah* itself, which as we have learned, reveals God as the eternal, self-existent One, the God of revelation, the God of moral and spiritual attributes—of righteousness, holiness, love, and therefore of redemption, the God who stands in special covenant relation to Israel in contrast to Elohim, the general name of God in relation to all the nations.

Most of these compound names of God arise out of some historic incident, and portray Jehovah in some aspect of His character as meeting human need.

HISTORICAL SETTING

The historic incident out of which the name *Jehovah-jireh* rises is one of the most moving and significant in the Word of God. The story is found in Genesis 22. It is the story of the last and greatest crisis in the life of Abraham. Every event in his life has led up to this supreme hour from the time of his call to a high destiny, through every vicissitude, through every joy, through every trial or failure, through every measure of success and blessing, through every hope and promise and assurance. All had been in preparation for this event. The great promise had been fulfilled, the supreme hope of his life realized. He had settled down to live the rest of his life in peace and in joyous anticipation of the larger fulfillment of the promise through the centuries, and its final spiritual fulfillment. The rationalistic critics have long been silenced who denied or doubted the reality of the Patriarchs as actual persons, but interpreted them merely as ideal and imaginary figures around which ancient Hebrew tradition cast its national origins and early history. For apart from our faith in the Bible as the inspired revelation of God, and its Old and New Testament testimony, to the reality of Abraham as a historic person, abundant evidence has been brought to light in recent years and decades as to the historicity of the persons and the veracity of the events to dispel all doubts and invalidate all objections.

In this incident *Elohim* appears to Abraham with the astounding command to offer up as a sacrifice, a burnt offering, his only and well-beloved son Isaac. Abraham, apparently, is not aware that this is a testing. His feelings can scarcely be imagined. His tremendous faith, in view of all the circumstances, is, perhaps, not sufficiently appreciated. The record reveals not a word of objection or remonstrance on his part. But if he laughed in his heart with joyful hope, even though perhaps mingled with a little doubt, when this son was promised to him, how deep his anguish and perplexity must have been at this amazing request from the God who had been so good to him. Yet the faith which enabled him to believe such a staggering promise in the first place is now sufficient for an even more staggering demand. This incident, then, reveals Abraham's obedience and faith,

Isaac's willing submission, and *Jehovah's* gracious provision of a substitute in his place.

THE MEANING OF THE NAME

Before we discuss the derivation and meaning of this name, it will be well to briefly recall the happenings which occasioned its use. On the way to the place of sacrifice Isaac cannot contain his curiosity about the lamb for the burnt offering. "Behold the fire and wood"; he said, "but where is the lamb for a burnt offering?" (Gen. 22:7). Abraham's answer to this question is that God will provide Himself a lamb. It is not necessary to suppose that Abraham thought of an ordinary lamb in this answer, although he may have had some such dim hope in his mind. At any rate, in his instructions to his young men to wait for him he says: "I and the lad will go yonder and worship, and come again to you" (v. 5). It is only at the last moment, when Isaac lies bound upon the altar, and any such hope he may have entertained is gone, and the knife in his upraised hand is about to descend, that the voice of the angel of Jehovah arrests and stays his hand, and Abraham looks about and sees a ram caught in a thicket by its horns, which he offers up instead of his son. Then in verse 14 we read in the Authorized Version of our Bible: "And Abraham called the name of that place Jehovah-jireh: as it is said to this day, In the mount of the Lord [Jehovah] it shall be seen." In the American Standard Version of our Bible, however, instead of "it shall be seen," it reads "it shall be provided." Still another rendering of this important word is "he shall be seen." Thus, "in the mount of Jehovah, he shall be seen or provided."

First of all it must be understood that in this name Jehovah-jireh, the word *jireh* is simply a transliteration of a Hebrew word which appears many times throughout the Scriptures and is translated for what it means. Only its unusual significance here, its connection with this remarkable event, and its union with the title *Jehovah* has brought it down to us as a compound name of God. It is simply a form of the verb *to see.* What connection can there be then between the word *see* and *provide,* for both of these English words are used to translate the one Hebrew word, and they certainly seem to be quite distinct in their meaning? It must be admitted, too, that in the great majority of cases where this word occurs in the Hebrew Bible, it is translated "see" or "appear." Why then should we translate it "provide" here?

One reason for this, no doubt, as one writer declares,[1] is, that with God, to see is also to foresee. As the One who possesses eternal wisdom and knowledge, He knows the end from the beginning. As Elohim He is all-knowing, all-wise, and all-powerful. From eternity to eternity He foresees everything. But another word for seeing is *vision,* from the Latin word *video*—to see. Thus with God foreseeing is prevision. As the Jehovah of righteousness and holiness, and of love and redemption, having prevision of man's sin, and fall, and need, He makes provision for that need. For provision, after all, is merely a compound of two Latin words meaning "to see beforehand." And we may learn from a dictionary that *provide* is simply the verb and *prevision* the noun of seeing beforehand. Thus to God prevision is necessarily followed by provision, for He certainly will pro-

---

[1] Webb-Peploe, *The Titles of Jehovah,* p. 24.

vide for that need which His foreseeing shows Him to exist. With Him prevision and provision are one and the same thing. All this is certainly expressed in the term *Jehovah-jireh;* and it is quite correct and in its proper significance to translate this name of God *Jehovah jireh,* "God will provide."

Another form of the word from which *jireh* is derived is also used of men in the sense of foresee. It is translated "seer" or "prophet." Several references are made in the Scriptures to Samuel the Seer and the Book of Samuel the Seer (I Chron. 9:22; 26:28; II Sam. 15:27; II Chron. 16:7). The word is *ro'eh* which, as can easily be seen, is much like *jireh.* In I Samuel 9:9 it is stated that the prophet formerly was called a seer. Even as late as the time of Isaiah (30:10) this was the word sometimes used for a prophet. Here the prophet Isaiah speaks of a people who say to the seers: "See not; and to the prophets, Prophesy not unto us right things." A prophet is, of course, one who foresees, and since *seer,* or *ro'eh,* is the same as *prophet,* it consequently means one who foresees.

Besides this the word *jireh* is translated in Genesis 22:8, even in our Authorized Version of the Bible, as *provide.* Abraham here said to Isaac: "My son, God will provide himself a lamb for a burnt offering." Even if we were to translate here, "God will see to it," or "God will see for Himself a lamb for a burnt offering," the meaning would be exactly the same as *provide.*

The importance of the words used here can hardly be overestimated, and afford striking evidence and confirmation of the hand of God in revelation. "Abraham called the name of the place Jehovah-jireh: as it is said to this day, In the mount of the Lord it or he shall be seen." "It shall be seen"—*jeroeh*—the same word as *jireh*. That is, God's provision shall be seen. In the mount of the Lord! What was this mount of the Lord? In Genesis 22:2 the command comes to Abraham: "Take now thy son, thine only son Isaac, whom thou lovest, and get thee into the land of Moriah; and offer him there upon one of the mountains which I will tell thee of." The significant word here is the word *Moriah*, of which more will be said later. This word, many Hebrew scholars agree, is a kindred word to *jireh*, derived from the same root. Its ending is an abbreviated form of the name *Jehovah*. Thus it may be rendered "seen" or "provided of Jehovah." All of this confirms and justifies our translation of the word *jireh* as "seeing" or "appearing and providing," and invests this name of Jehovah with a wealth of meaning and significance.

THE SIGNIFICANCE OF THIS NAME

This name is significant, first of all, because it is a commemoration—a commemoration of a great deliverance. This was the primary reason for naming the scene of this event Jehovah-jireh. It was a constant reminder of the wonderful grace of the Jehovah who had wrought this deliverance. Now that it was all over, and Abraham had learned the lesson God was teaching him and could see something of God's glorious purpose in it all, he sought only to magnify the grace of Jehovah. His magnifying of this grace was in proportion to the deep and dark perplexity that had filled his soul on the way to the mount. Had God really spoken to him and called him? Did the Elohim mean what He had said? Could He really mean what He said now? Such may have been Abraham's thoughts. But his joy and gratitude were in proportion to his sorrow and despair at the terrible prospect before him—the overwhelming horror that must have flooded his soul at the thought, yes, the very act of plunging the knife of sacrifice into the body of his own son, his only son, the son so longed for, hoped for, prayed for, the child of their old age. What a great and glorious deliverance it was that Jehovah's grace had provided, and how unexpected and dramatic! Man's extremity is ever God's opportunity, not only for deliverance but to teach also wonderful lessons of His purpose as well as providence.

Surely out of this experience of Jehovah's delivering grace there must have come a purer, more spiritual relationship of love between this father and son. This must have been one lesson the experience was intended to convey. As one great commentator has declared, it was that he should no more love his beloved son as his flesh and blood, but solely and only as the gracious gift and possession of God, as a good entrusted to him by God; which he was to be ready to render back to Him at any moment (Delitzsch). According to the words of the angel of Jehovah it is fullest proof of Abraham's faith and obedience, "seeing thou hast not withheld thy son, thine only son from me." And He might have added, "Even as I will not withhold my only and well-beloved Son as the great provision for man's redemption." For this, after all, is the chief lesson of the story, the deliverance of Isaac through the provision of a substitute. For just as Abraham is about to slay him, the voice of the angel of Jehovah arrests him: "Lay not thine hand upon the lad, neither do anything unto him." And there in the thicket is the substitute provided by Jehovah.

A further significance of this name of God lies in the expectation of something yet to come. Even if we were to translate *Jehovah-jireh* as "the Lord doth provide" rather than *"will* provide," it would be Abraham's testimony to the fact that Jehovah is a God who always provides; that as He provided then He would also provide in the future—deliverance from death, the oil of joy for the ashes of sorrow and mourning, blessings for obedience, even though obedience be made perfect through sufferings. The naming of the place Jehovah-jireh was meant to be proverbial of this very thing—"as it is said to this day."

But this naming of the place was more than proverbial with Abraham. He can hardly have emerged from such a remarkable and solemn experience without feeling or realizing that it had far deeper significance than the test of his own faith only. The profound import of the occasion is strikingly attested by the most solemn language of Jehovah Himself calling from heaven a second time after the lamb of His provision had been offered, and saying, "By myself have I sworn, saith Jehovah." The word translated "saith" is the particular word used of Jehovah when making the most solemn prophetic utterances. Some translate it "utterance," others, "oracle." Then follows an emphatic confirmation of the promises to make Abraham a multitude, and a blessing to the world "because thou hast done this thing," and "because thou hast obeyed my voice." There are various allusions in the New Testament to this great transaction that indicate that Abraham saw far more than the immediate provision and deliverance in it. It was more than proverbial. He saw in it a prediction. He called the name of the place Jehovah-jireh; not merely

Jehovah doth provide but Jehovah will provide. And then, "as it is said to this day, In the mount of Jehovah it shall be seen" or "it shall be provided." One of the most noted of medieval Jewish commentators also understood this expression to mean, "God will manifest Himself to His people."

THE REALIZATION

What then was that provision which Abraham saw, dimly perhaps, with the eye of faith? What was the reality of which Isaac, and the lamb, were but types? Certainly Abraham understood the reality of sin, and realized the need for atonement. The numerous altars he built and the offerings he sacrificed attest that fact. Why then the demand for Isaac as an offering? Was it not to impress upon Abraham more deeply the temporary character of these sacrifices; that it was impossible that the blood of bulls and goats should take away sins (Heb. 10:4); that they were only shadows of which something infinitely worthier should be the substance and reality? Thus Isaac was exhibited as the pattern of one under the judgment of God for sin. Animals cannot take away the sins of men. Animals cannot be consecrated to God instead of men. "Lebanon is not sufficient to burn, nor the beasts thereof sufficient for a burnt offering" (Isa. 40:16). Only one of like nature, if one worthy enough can be found, can make such atonement and consecration. Here again in the deliverance of Isaac as he was about to be offered Abraham received more than an inkling of the fact that not even Isaac, that none born of flesh alone, is sufficient for that. For Isaac was offered and received back only in a figure (Heb. 11:19), and the lamb became his substitute also.

Surely God was teaching Abraham that the only sacrifice acceptable to Him is the one chosen and appointed by Himself. "Wherewithal shall I come before the Lord, and bow myself before the high God? Shall I come before him with burnt offerings, with calves of a year old? Will the Lord be pleased with thousands of rams . . . shall I give my first-born for my transgression, the fruit of my body for the sin of my soul?" says Micah 6:6, 7.

In the mount of the Lord it shall be seen or provided, and that mount is Moriah which, as already stated, means appearance or provision of God. It was this Mount Moriah which later became the site of the Temple and the center of Israel's worship, its sacrificial system. In II Chronicles 3:1 it is written: "Then Solomon began to build the house of the Lord [Jehovah] at Jerusalem in mount Moriah, where Jehovah appeared unto David his father, in the place that David had prepared in the threshing floor of Ornan, the Jebusite." It was here, in David's time, that God in His mercy staved the hand of avenging justice when David offered the sacrifices of substitution. The very heart of Israel's religion, centered in the Temple on Mount Moriah, was its substitutionary sacrifices. A Jewish interpretation of Genesis 22:14 is: "God will see and choose that very place to cause His Shekinah to rest thereon and to offer the offerings."

But, like Abraham, the true and faithful Israelite must have realized that the sacrifice of animals was only a shadow of something to come. Jehovah's gracious promise to Solomon in II Chronicles 7 to set His heart and eyes and His glory on that place indicate something infinitely nobler than animal sacrifice.

Isaiah and Micah make sublime predictions concerning the mountain of the house of the Lord. Zechariah speaks of the glory of that holy mountain, the mountain of Jehovah of hosts. What was the glory of that mountain? Surely it was no temple made with hands! Surely it was not all the beasts on Jewish altars slain. The Abraham who looked not for an earthly city but for one "which hath foundations, whose builder and maker is God," also looked for a better and more enduring sacrifice; for the Mount Moriah of which he spoke saying: "In the mount of the Lord it shall be seen," became the site of Calvary and the scene of that grand and awful sacrifice of God's only begotten and well-beloved Son, who was put under judgment for sin, and became our Substitute. Perhaps Abraham understood better than we realize the wonder of Jehovah's provision for man's redemption when he said: "In the Mount of Jehovah, he will appear." Was it not this to which the Lord Jesus Christ Himself referred in John 8:56, when He said: "Your father Abraham rejoiced to see my day: and he saw it, and was glad."

Abraham and Isaac, as father and only begotten son, are both types of Jehovah's full and glorious provision for man's sin and need. "God so loved the world that he gave his only begotten Son . . ." (John 3:16). And Paul speaks of God as "he that spared not his own Son, but delivered him up for us all . . ." (Rom. 8:32). "Who was delivered up for our trespasses . . ." (Rom. 4:25). And John says again: "In this was manifested the love of God toward us, in that God sent his only begotten Son into the world, that we might live through him" (I John 4:9).

On Mount Moriah Jehovah was teaching Abraham what He Himself was prepared to provide. He was teaching the awful cost to Himself of the provision of the sacrifice for sin. Does it break your heart, Abraham, to give up, to slay, yes, by your own hand, as an innocent sacrifice, your well-beloved and only son? Then think of the awful and infinite cost to *Me* of what *I* am prepared to do for man. The thing that Abraham foreshadowed on Mount Moriah was realized, accomplished, when God's Son upon the cross cried, "It is finished."

Isaac asks, "Where is the lamb?" Abraham answers, "God will provide himself a lamb." John the Baptist announces, "Behold the Lamb of God, which taketh away the sin of the world" (John 1:29). This was the Lamb provided and slain from the foundation of the world but manifested on Mount Moriah for us; through whose precious blood, even the blood of Christ, as of a lamb without blemish and without spot, we are redeemed (I Peter 1:18, 19). This Lamb is the center of heaven's glory and the object of its adoration. Ten thousand times ten thousand, and thousands of thousands say with a loud voice: "Worthy is the Lamb that was slain to receive power, and riches, and wisdom, and might, and honor, and glory and blessing." Yes, and every creature will join in saying: "Blessing and honor, and glory, and power, be unto him that sitteth upon the throne, and unto the Lamb forever and ever" (Rev. 5:11-13).

God will provide Himself a lamb. In the mount of the Lord it shall be seen, it shall be provided. In the mount of the Lord He was seen, He was provided, even Jesus

Christ, the Lamb of God, our Saviour, our Lord, to whom be glory forever, and who is over all God blessed forever. Amen.

6

JEHOVAH-ROPHE

THE NAME *Jehovah-rophe* means Jehovah heals. It is the second of the compound names of Jehovah. The name *Jehovah-jireh* arose out of the incident of Jehovah's provision of a substitute in place of Isaac whom He had commanded Abraham to sacrifice upon the altar. We learned that it stands for Jehovah's great provision for man's redemption in the sacrifice of His only begotten Son, our Lord Jesus Christ, who was the Lamb of God who taketh away the sin of the world, and who was offered up on the very spot where Abraham had predicted—"In the mount of the Lord it shall be seen" —that is, Mount Moriah in Jerusalem, the scene of Calvary.

There is a wonderful and significant order in these compound names of Jehovah as they appear in the Scriptures (in contrast to the waste and desolation which certain critics have wrought upon the Scriptures; whose "assured results" have only obscured the light for those who accept them). In these names there is a progressive revelation of Jehovah meeting every need as it arises in the experience of His redeemed people—saving, sustaining, strengthening, sanctifying, and so on; and not only for the redeemed of that day but for God's saints in all ages. The things that happened to Israel, the apostle Paul tells us, were our examples (I Cor. 10:6).

70

"Now all these things happened unto them for ensamples: and they are written for our admonition, upon whom the ends of the world are come," he again remarks in I Corinthians 10:11.

For this name of God, Jehovah-rophe, arises out of one of Israel's earliest experiences in the wilderness as told in Exodus 15:22-26. Indeed it was their first experience after the crossing of the Red Sea and the singing of the great song of triumph. But the same chapter which records Israel's triumphant song also records the first murmurings of discontent and bitterness. In Exodus 15:22 we read: "So Moses brought Israel from the Red sea, and they went out into the wilderness of Shur; and they went three days in the wilderness, and found no water." In the first flush of victory they went along joyfully the first day, and perhaps even the second day. But the way was hot and weary, and their water was giving out. The third day was well along and still there was no water. Their throats were parched. They felt their plight bcoming desperate. They forgot the might and mercy of the God who had so marvelously delivered them. In their anxiety and anger they murmured against Moses in bitter complaint. Then in verse 23: "And when they came to Marah, they could not drink of the waters of Marah, for they were bitter: therefore the name of it was called Marah" (which means bitter). We can imagine their feelings of relief and joy as they first came in sight of this well, but what angry disillusionment when they find the waters bitter—an aggravation and a mockery of their thirst. They were maddened by this setback to their hope and expectation. What were they to do? Were they and their children to die there of thirst? Then God showed Moses a certain tree, which, when cast into the waters, turned them from bitterness to sweetness so that the people drank. They were refreshed and strengthened and heartened for the journey ahead. Their murmuring was turned to praise as their confidence in Jehovah and His servant Moses was renewed.

But it was not God who was there on trial. It was the people. He was proving them, and saying to them (v. 26): "If thou wilt diligently hearken to the voice of Jehovah thy God, and wilt do that which is right in his sight . . . I will put none of these diseases upon thee, which I have brought upon the Egyptians: *for I am Jehovah that healeth thee*"—that is, Jehovah-rophecha. The word *rophe* appears some sixty or seventy times in the Old Testament, always meaning to restore, to heal, to cure, or a physician, not only in the physical sense but in the moral and spiritual sense also. As out of Abraham's trying experience in the mount there came a new and comforting name of God, Jehovah-jireh, so out of Israel's bitter experience in the wilderness there comes another new and comforting name of God, Jehovah-rophe, Jehovah heals. And Jehovah here pledged Himself on condition of their obedience to be always their Healer.

MAN'S NEED OF HEALING

Perhaps the first lesson we may draw from this story, since these events are all examples to us, is humanity's need of healing, of a physician—even in a physical sense. The Old Testament reveals a number of instances in which God's power is manifested, even though sometimes by natural means, to heal the bodies of men. A notable instance is that of King Hezekiah who was not only healed but granted a definite additional span of years to live.

Nothing is more obvious and tragic and costly than the toll which sickness has exacted from human life and happiness. Disease is rife and often rampant the world over and has wrought untold havoc. It is no respecter of persons and stretches out its tentacles into all classes and communities and climes. It is a grim fact of human existence with which mankind has always had to cope and which has called for the exercise of its best brains, and effort, and resourcefulness. Terrible plagues and scourges have at times threatened the existence of an entire continent and have actually destroyed large portions of populations. Yes, mankind is physically sick and is in constant need of a physician, of healing. According to the Old Testament, God, Himself the one who heals, has used sickness and disease present in the earth as an instrument of judgment upon sin. For David's sin against Him, God offers him the choice of one of three punishments. The responsibility of the terrible choice involved is so great that David simply places it in the hands of God who chooses to bring pestilence (I Chron. 21:12-14). The many hospitals and asylums and institutions everywhere, built and maintained at great cost, bear witness to the prevalence and tragedy of sickness in the world. What a mass of disease and sickness upon the earth when the Great Physician walked upon it in the flesh. Healing is certainly a great and noble and effective part of the missionary enterprise of the Church. How appropriate to the physical need of men is the name Jehovah-rophe!

But man's need of healing is even greater in the moral and spiritual realm. For here the ravages of sin are even more grim and obvious. The tragedy and sorrow and pain and woe are even greater. In a figure of the physical the prophet Isaiah describes the moral and spiritual condition of his own people: "The whole head is sick, and the whole heart faint. From the sole of the foot even unto the head there is no soundness in it; but wounds, and bruises, and putrefying sores: they have not been closed, neither bound up, neither mollified with ointment" (Isa. 1:5, 6). The moral and spiritual sickness of mankind is an open, running sore. The heart of man is desperately sick, says Jeremiah (17:9). Herein is its fundamental disease—the sin which alienates it from God—the sin which manifests itself in open and secret evil of every sort, in high places and in low, which brought the judgment of Jehovah in times of old, and ever since, and must yet. How sorely mankind is in need of a healer, a physician! The world lies in the bitterness and bond of iniquity.

It is like the waters of Marah to which the children of Israel came in the wilderness. It is not sweetness and life but bitterness and death. Yet the antidote to its poison, the remedy for its sickness, is ever near—even at hand, as it was near the waters of Marah. For there God performed His miracle of healing by means of a tree growing nearby. It was the tree of God cast into the waters there that healed and sweetened them.

Jehovah the Healer in the Old Testament

This brings us to the second point, that Jehovah is the great Healer of men. He alone has the remedy that can heal the spirits of men. He is the remedy for the healing of man. And the Gospel is concerned primarily and chiefly with the moral and spiritual sickness and healing of mankind, for behind all the evils and physical sickness is sin. The importance of Marah in Israel's and human experience is attested by the fact that God gave Himself this new name here—Jehovah, who heals. The significance of the name *Jehovah* must be recalled here as "used in connection with beings who can apprehend and appreciate the Infinite." Therefore this name first appears in connection with His dealings with men. We learned that the title *Jehovah* and its use suggest moral and spiritual attributes in God—righteousness, holiness, love; that He holds man, created in the image of God, responsible for such moral and spiritual qualities. Man's sin and fall therefore called forth the judgment of Jehovah. But the love of Jehovah triumphs over judgment in providing a redemption, as we saw in the name *Jehovah-jireh*. So, too, the One who heals from the sin which mars and corrupts mankind is again Jehovah, as distinguished from His other names.

Now Marah may stand for disappointment and bitter experiences in the life of God's children, who have been redeemed, as was Israel in Egypt through the Passover Lamb, and snatched by divine power from the terrible pursuing enemy; who meet, like Israel at Marah, with severe testing and trial, and in their disappointment and discouragement sometimes murmur with a bitter and faithless complaint, forgetting the great salvation and power of God. Certainly Marah stands for the sweetening of those bitternesses, the curing of the ills to which both flesh and spirit are heir. True, God has implanted healing properties in waters and drugs even to the present day for the healing of bodily ills. He has made man capable of wresting secrets from nature which have marvelously advanced the art of healing. It is true that His is the healing hand behind it all. But this incident is intended chiefly as a lesson and warning against that sin and disobedience which lie at the root of all sorrow, suffering, and sickness in the world. The tree there cast into the waters is obviously a figure of the tree on which hung the Jehovah of the New Testament—even Jesus, the only remedy for the cure of mankind's ills—and which alone can sweeten the bitterness of human experience through that forgiveness of sin and sanctifying of life which it accomplished.

Certainly God could and did heal physical maladies in the Old Testament whenever it pleased Him. Moses cried out to Jehovah in behalf of Miriam smitten with leprosy: "Heal her now, O God, I beseech thee" (Num. 12:13). The Old Testament clearly reveals God's anxious desire and purpose to heal the hurt of His people, and the wounds and sorrows of all mankind. Certainly God removed plagues and pestilences. But the fact that He visited such plagues and pestilences as punishment is evidence of the underlying root of it all— sin. The psalmist acknowledges this when he says: "Bless the Lord, O my soul . . . who [first] forgiveth all thine iniquities and [then] healeth all thy diseases" (Ps. 103:2, 3).

Other Scriptures state this even more strongly. "Why criest thou for thine affliction? Thy sorrow is incurable for the multitude of thine iniquity; because thy sins were increased, I have done these things unto thee" (Jer. 30:15). "Hast thou utterly rejected Judah? Hath thy soul loathed Zion? Why hast thou smitten us, and there is no healing for us? We looked for peace, and there is no good; and for the time of healing, and behold trouble!

We acknowledge, O Lord, our wickedness, and the iniquity of our fathers: for we have sinned against thee" (Jer. 14:19, 20).

Then many references to sickness and wounds are simply figurative expressions of moral and spiritual ills, so that it is rather in this sense that God is known as Jehovah-rophe—Jehovah who heals. This is what Jeremiah means when he says: "For I will restore health unto thee, and I will heal thee of thy wounds, saith Jehovah" (30:17); and again: "Return, ye backsliding children and I will heal your backslidings" (3:22). So Isaiah speaks of the day in which "Jehovah bindeth up the breach of his people, and healeth the stroke of their wound" (30:26). He predicts the coming of One upon whom the Spirit of Jehovah God will rest in order, among other things, to bind up the brokenhearted (61:1).

The will, and the power, and the longing are present in Jehovah to heal. The only obstacle in the way is man himself. The remedy is there—near at hand—as near as the tree at Marah's waters. "The word is very nigh unto thee, in thy mouth, and in thy heart," says Moses (Deut. 30:14). There is salvation for every sin, healing for every evil. The remedy only awaits acknowledgment or application. This, man has often been unwilling to do. A king of Judah smitten with a disease, evidently and appropriately because of a certain evil act, sought not to the Lord, but to the physicians (II Chron. 16:12). It was because of sin that the remedy lay for him in Jehovah's hand alone, even though physicians may have been sufficient for the cure otherwise. For the hurt of his people, brought about by sin, Jeremiah asks: "Is there no balm in Gilead; is there no physician there? Why then is not the health of the daughter of my people recovered?" (Jer. 8:21, 22). The remedy was there—in Jehovah Himself—but they went on and on refusing it "till there was no remedy" (or healing) (II Chron. 36:16). And centuries later the word of the Lord Jesus to His people was, "Ye will not come to me, that ye might have life" (John 5:40).

JESUS THE HEALER IN THE NEW TESTAMENT

The Jehovah who heals in the Old Testament is the Jesus who heals in the New.

The ministry of the Lord Jesus began with healing. In the synagogue at Nazareth, having returned in the power of the Spirit from His great temptation, He opened His public ministry by quoting Isaiah 61:1: "The Spirit of the Lord is upon me, because he hath anointed me to preach the gospel to the poor; he hath sent me to heal the brokenhearted, to preach deliverance to the captives, and recovering of sight to the blind, to set at liberty them that are bruised" (Luke 4:18). In Luke 4:23 we find Him saying to them: "Ye will surely say unto me this proverb, Physician, heal thyself: Whatsoever we have heard done in Capernaum, do also here in thy country." The reference was to acts of healing which the Lord Jesus had performed there. In the same chapter various acts of healing are recorded—the healing of fevers, the cleansing of leprosy, the casting out of demons. So He continued all through His ministry. They brought to Him all that were diseased. And He went about "teaching in their synagogues, and preaching the gospel of the kingdom, and healing all manner of sickness and all manner of disease among the people"

(Matt. 4:23). These miracles of healing constantly amazed the people and He cited them as proofs of His identity and mission. When John in prison doubts His identity, He sends back word: "Go and show John again those things which ye do hear and see: the blind receive their sight, and the lame walk, the lepers are cleansed, and the deaf hear, the dead are raised up, and the poor have the gospel preached to them" (Matt. 11:4, 5). "The same works that I do bear witness of me, that the Father hath sent me," He said (John 5:36).

But as with Jehovah of the Old, so with Jesus of the New Testament, physical healing was only incidental to His chief object, which was the healing of the souls of men. His opening words in the synagogue at Nazareth declared His mission to be to preach the Gospel, to preach deliverance, to set at liberty. His miracles of healing were proof of His identity and mission—His credentials. Healing men's bodies was a great and blessed work, indeed. Yet many of the sicknesses He healed were striking symptoms of that dark, dread disease which has its roots in the soul of men and not in the body—the disease of sin. How often He cast out demons! And what does demon-possession stand for but sin-possession? How often He healed the leper! And what is leprosy but a type of sin in its foulness and vileness. The Old Testament is clearest in its teaching of this truth. How often He said to those He healed, "Sin no more!" or "Thy sins be forgiven thee!" And He silences His carping critics and accusers with the words: "They that be whole need not a physician, but they that are sick" (Matt. 9:12); and connecting the idea of sickness and healing with sin, He continues: "for I am not come to call the righteous, but sinners to repent-

ance" (Matt. 9:13). True, He went about healing
bodies and doing good, but His invitation ever was:
"Come unto me and I will give you rest"—"rest [or
cure] unto your souls."

Then the Lord Jesus consummated His ministry by
becoming that tree which made the bitter pools of human existence waters of life and healing and sweetness.
The teaching of Marah is wonderfully fulfilled in Him.
There they were taught the corruption and the bitterness
of the purely natural waters which are only an aggravation of the soul's sickness and need. Only the tree of
God's provision and choice could purify and sweeten
and satisfy. To the woman at the well the Lord Jesus
said: "Whosoever drinketh of this water shall thirst
again: but whosoever drinketh of the water that I shall
give him shall never thirst; but the water that I shall give
him shall be in him a well of water springing up into
everlasting life" (John 4:13, 14). On a great feast day
in the Temple at Jerusalem He cried: "If any man
thirst, let him come unto me and drink. He that believeth on me, as the scripture hath said, from within him
shall flow rivers of living water" (John 7:37, 38,
A.S.V.). The Lord Jesus is both the tree and the waters.
"Who his own self bare our sins in his own body on
the tree, that we, being dead to sins, should live unto
righteousness; by whose stripes ye were healed." He is
the Well of salvation (Isa. 12:3), the Water of life,
sweet, saving and satisfying.

In Him the tree of life and the river of life in Eden's
garden are free and accessible once more to Adam's
sons. This is the picture presented to us in the closing
scene of the Book of Revelation: "And he showed me a
pure river of water of life, clear as crystal, proceeding

out of the throne of God and of the Lamb. In the midst of the street of it, and on either side of the river, was there the tree of life, which bare twelve manner of fruits, and yielded her fruit every month: and the leaves of the tree were for the healing of the nations" (Rev. 22:1, 2).

The Word of Jehovah which He spoke by His messenger, the prophet Malachi, has found glorious fulfillment and awaits a yet more glorious fulfillment. "But unto you that fear my name shall the Sun of righteousness arise with healing in his wings" (Mal. 4:2). What Jehovah was to Israel at Marah, so the Lord Jesus is to all who will receive and obey Him, the Great Physician. How sad, that, like Israel of old who refused Jehovah till there was no remedy, multitudes today have refused the healing sacrifice and ministry of Jehovah-Jesus! And along with many who call themselves by His name, they prefer other physicians and remedies to Him—culture, science, philosophy, social improvement—forgers of lies and physicians of no value, as Job calls them (13:4). But praise God for the multitudes who have received Him, and applied His remedy, and have been made whole, and "take the water of life freely" (Rev. 22:17).

7

JEHOVAH-NISSI

AND MOSES BUILT AN ALTAR, and called the name of it
Jehovah-nissi [Jehovah, my banner]" (Exod. 17:15).

Only a few weeks had elapsed from the time the children of Israel left Marah, the place of bitter waters, till
they reached Rephidim, the scene of Jehovah's revelation of Himself to them as Jehovah-nissi, Jehovah my
banner. At Marah, we will recall, in healing the bitter
waters of that place, He had revealed Himself as Jehovah-rophe, Jehovah who heals, the one who alone has
the remedy for the sins of mankind, the balm for the
sorrows and sufferings of His people; who has sweetened the bitter waters of human misery and death
through Christ, the Tree of life and the sweet and living
waters.

The children of Israel had gone from Marah to Elim,
the place of refreshing and rest (Exod. 15:27). From
there they journeyed to the wilderness of Sin (Exod.
16) where they murmured against Moses because there
was no food, and where they longed for the fleshpots of
Egypt. There, Jehovah appeared in the cloud of glory
and began to feed them with the wilderness manna.
Then they came to Rephidim where there was no water
(Exod. 17). At Marah the waters were bitter. Here there
was no water at all. "And the people thirsted there for
water." Hunger is difficult and discouraging enough to

82

bear, but the sufferings and torments of thirst are unbearable. Their murmurings and threatenings against Moses were rather a tempting of Jehovah. They doubted God. Forgotten, the marvelous passage of the Red Sea and the drowning of Pharaoh and his hosts; forgotten, the miraculous healing of Marah's waters! Ignoring the coming down of the manna from heaven, they questioned God's goodness and even His presence. "Is the Lord among us, or not?" they said. And there from the rock in Horeb, that rock which Paul tells us was Christ (I Cor. 10:4), Jehovah caused waters to spring forth to quench the multitude's thirst.

Then came the experience which occasioned Jehovah's revelation of Himself to His people as Jehovah-nissi. Israel discovered that perhaps there were worse enemies than even hunger and thirst. They now learned that their pathway was to be contested and barred by implacable human foes. For "then came Amalek, and fought with Israel in Rephidim" (Exod. 17:8).

ISRAEL'S ENEMY

Who were the Amalekites?

The Amalekites were the descendants of Amalek, a grandson of Esau, we are told in Genesis 36:12. Thus they were direct descendants of Isaac. Yet they became the persistent and hereditary enemies of Israel, a thorn in the flesh, and a constant menace to their spiritual and national life. Balaam calls them "the first of the nations" (Num. 24:20), that is, to oppose Israel. They were a numerous and powerful people. It might have been expected that, as closely related to Israel as they were, they would have afforded help instead of opposition. Yet they opposed Israel in a most mean and cowardly way. Years later Moses calls upon Israel to "remember what Amalek did unto thee by the way as ye came forth out of Egypt; how he met thee by the way, and smote the hindmost of thee, all that were feeble behind thee, when thou wast faint and weary; and he feared not God" (Deut. 25:17, 18). God had bidden him write in a book the words: "For I will utterly put out the remembrance of Amalek from under heaven" and "Jehovah hath sworn that Jehovah will have war with Amalek from generation to generation" (Exod. 17:14-16). For "the face of Jehovah is against them that do evil, to cut off their memory from the earth."

Centuries later Samuel came to King Saul with a commission from Jehovah to utterly destroy the Amalekites with all their possessions so that not a trace of them or theirs should remain (I Sam. 15:3). The failure of King Saul to carry out the command to destroy Amalek (I Sam. 15:2, 3) led to his own rejection and death (I Sam. 15:26-28). When he lay mortally wounded on the battlefield of Mount Gilboa, a young man, a stranger, came to him. Saul urgently requested this young man to put an end to him for he knew he could not live, and did not wish to fall into the hands of his conquerors while yet alive (II Sam. 1:1-16). By the bitter irony of a just retribution this young man was an Amalekite. The sinful thing which Saul had spared now returned to slay him. Not until the days of King Hezekiah was the command finally carried out, that "the rest of the Amalekites that were escaped were smitten" (I Chron. 4:43). This is no doubt one reason why Hezekiah was so favored by Jehovah. Yet it is highly probable that the Haman, who a thousand years after Moses almost accomplished the total destruction of all the Jews in Persia, as told in the Book of Esther—Haman the Agagite, as he is called—was a descendant of King Agag of the Amalekites, whom Saul in his foolish disobedience sought to spare alive.

The Amalekites were at that time living with their flocks and herds in the vicinity of Rephidim. Moved by suspicion, jealousy, and fear they resented the presence of such a multitude of strange people in the wilderness and were determined to prevent their passage through it. Thus they opposed the purpose and plan of God. They had first carried on a sort of harassing, guerilla campaign against Israel. Then apparently they came out against them in open, pitched battle.

ISRAEL'S TRIUMPH

Strange to say, there appears to have been no fear or confusion among Israel in such a crisis. Perhaps the recent miracle of the water from the rock had overawed them and inspired them with confidence and trust. Perhaps it was easier to fight a tangible foe of flesh and blood after the terrors of the wilderness with its hunger and thirst and weariness. At any rate, no hint is given of alarm or confusion. Moses calmly orders Joshua to choose men and go out and fight Amalek. These enemies of God's people, the masters of this peninsula of Sinai, thought, no doubt, to prevail easily over this newly freed slave rabble without supplies, without arms, without knowledge of the country. For Israel was indeed an ill-equipped, ill-disciplined, inexperienced mob going out against a well-armed and experienced foe. But Amalek little knew the secret source of the calm and courage of God's people. Two other factors, at least, must have contributed to this confidence. The first is the man Joshua, whom Moses chose to lead the expedition, a man of inflexible purpose, of indomitable courage, an able leader and soldier. His name had originally been Hoshea, a prince of the tribe of Ephraim (Num. 13:8). Hoshea means to give deliverance or help. But in Numbers 13:16 we read that Moses changed his name from Hoshea to Joshua, which means Jehovah is help or salvation. Whether this change was before or as a result of this event we do not know. But he must have been a man to inspire confidence and courage. And we know he was a man of faith, for he with Caleb were the only two of the twelve spies who brought back an encouraging report of the promised land they were sent to spy out. The second factor was, of course, Moses himself, now vindicated and honored in the eyes of the people after smiting the rock with his rod to bring the waters gushing out of it. In order to encourage Joshua and his men, Moses promises to take his position upon a hill with this rod, the rod of God, in his hand. In the account we are told that as long as Moses held up his hand, Israel prevailed, and when his hand was lowered Amalek prevailed. But Moses' hands were supported. Israel was finally victorious and the defeat of Amalek complete.

Moses standing upon the hill with uplifted hands has generally been thought of as interceding with God for the vindication of God's cause in the victory of His people. This factor of intercession suggested by the upraised hands was no doubt present and important in Moses' attitude. But there was something much more important than that, for in Moses' hand was the rod of God, the God-given rod, the wonder-working rod, the rod which brought the terrible plagues upon Egypt, which opened a path through the Red Sea for the deliverance of Israel, and brought the waters closing down in destruction on God's enemies. It was the rod of God's mighty hand and outstretched arm, the rod of the Elohim. How significant is this use of the name denoting His creative glory, might, and sovereignty, the general name of God, the name especially used in relationship to the nations (represented here by Amalek) as distinguished from Jehovah in relationship especially to Israel! Then it is the Elohim here, with the definite article, the only Elohim, denoting that whether Amalek acknowledged it or not, He was God.

It is this rod, as the banner of God, which brought the victory. What was the meaning then of Amalek's success when it was lowered and Israel's success when it was raised? It was to sharply emphasize and deeply impress upon Israel's warring soldiers and her watching, anxious host that upon God alone depended and to Him belonged the victory; that under His raised banner victory was always assured. No matter what the odds, then, for in Moses' own words five should chase a hundred and a hundred should chase ten thousand (Lev. 26:8). That rod was the symbol and pledge of His presence and power and working.

A banner, in ancient times, was not necessarily a flag such as we use nowadays. Often it was a bare pole with a bright shining ornament which glittered in the sun. The word here for banner means to glisten, among other things. It is translated variously pole, ensign, standard, and among the Jews it is also a word for miracle. As an ensign or standard it was a signal to God's people to rally to Him. It stood for His cause, His battle. It was a sign of deliverance, of salvation, as we shall see by the use of that word for the pole on which the brazen serpent was raised in the wilderness. It is the word used by the psalmist as "lift up" in the expression: "Lord, lift thou up the light of thy countenance upon us" (Ps. 4:6). So, *Joshua,* that is, Jehovah is salvation; the rod of Elohim held aloft in Moses' upraised hand as God's banner o'er them; and the light of His countenance upon them—these were Israel's victory.

THE WELFARE OF THE SAINTS

Israel our Example. Israel's experience of battle is the analogy of our own spiritual warfare. Amalek represents the forces of this world order which stand opposed to Jehovah in all ages, the rulers and princes of this world who have lifted up their standard against the Lord and against His anointed. Exodus 17:16 reads: "Jehovah hath sworn that Jehovah will have war with Amalek from generation to generation," but the original could bear the rendering: "For there is a hand upon or against the throne of Jehovah; Jehovah will have war against Amalek from generation to generation." It represented the world which lieth in the wicked one (I John 5:19). Its characteristics are the lust of the flesh, the lust of the eyes, and the pride of life (I John 2:16).

Amalek was a grandson of Esau, who despised spiritual things and preferred a mess of pottage to a spiritual birthright. He was the first enemy to appear to a redeemed people. Israel had just been redeemed, and baptized in the cloud and in the sea. They had partaken of that spiritual meat, represented by the manna, and drunk of that spiritual rock which was Christ, as represented by the waters of Horeb. The newly born believer at once finds the old man of the flesh confronting him in sharp contrast and opposition to the new man of the Spirit within him, "for the flesh lusteth against the Spirit, and the Spirit against the flesh: and these are contrary the one to the other" (Gal. 5:17). The apostle Paul declared that in the flesh there is no good thing (Rom. 7:18), and regarded it as a law in his members warring against his mind, and seeking to bring him into captivity to itself (Rom. 7:23). It is this flesh and its lusts which are to be crucified in those who are Christ's, His redeemed (Gal. 5:24).

The sphere of the conflict, however, as already indicated, is wider than that of the individual. Amalek may also be said to stand for the kingdoms of this world and their enmity to and attacks upon the people of God— against Israel of old and against the Church now. And the world is enmity to God. The kingdoms of this world are not yet become the kingdoms of our Lord and of His Christ (Rev. 11:15). There is a usurper upon the throne of these kingdoms, the same one who opposes and exalts himself above all that is called God (II Thess. 2:4); who once tempted the rightful King with the offer of these kingdoms if He would fall down and worship him (Matt. 4:8, 9). Amalek was, as already stated, simply the firstfruits of the heathen, the beginning of Gentile power and hostility to the people of God, representing the kingdom of darkness as against the kingdom of light, of evil against good, of a lie against the truth.

God is represented, especially as Jehovah of hosts, as lifting up a standard against the nations, of which Amalek is a type. "Lift ye up a banner upon the high mountain . . . I have commanded my sanctified ones, even them that rejoice in my highness. The noise of a multitude in the mountains, like as of a great people; a tumultuous noise of the kingdoms of nations gathered together: the Lord of hosts mustereth the host of the battle . . . I will punish the world for their evil, and the wicked for their iniquity" (Isa. 13:2-4, 11; Jer. 51:12, 27). But behind every outward manifestation the conflict is essentially spiritual. For the gates of Hell are ever assaulting the Church. And "we wrestle not against flesh and blood, but against principalities, against powers, against the rulers of the darkness of this world, against spiritual wickedness in high places" (Eph. 6:12).

Our participation in this warfare. There is a striking contrast between the experience at the Red Sea and the experience at Rephidim. At the Red Sea, the children of Israel, terrified at the sight of Pharaoh's hosts coming upon them, and the way of escape barred on every hand, were commanded not to do anything, but simply to "stand still, and see the salvation of Jehovah" (Exod. 14:13). For in the work of salvation God alone is the agent. God was here acting in redemption which is by grace, through faith alone, and not of works. They could do nothing to secure that salvation. But once having been delivered and introduced into a new life there appeared a warfare to be waged. They were to fight the good fight of faith which must ever be the experience of every serious believer. That there are very many who appear to think that nothing more is needed after the initial experience of redemption is all too obvious. The experience of Israel is to warn us against such a deadly fallacy. It is not now, stand still and see the salvation of God. That salvation has been accomplished. Moses

says to Joshua in clear, crisp commands: "Choose us
out men, and go out, fight with Amalek." Moses meant
business. Too many people do not. We are not saved by
works, but we are saved to works (Eph. 2:10) and to a
serious warfare. At Rephidim a redeemed people must
fight the good fight of faith (II Tim. 4:7). We are also
told to "earnestly contend for the faith" (Jude 3), although many have confused contend with contention.
We are to be good soldiers of Jesus Christ, willing to endure hardness, well pleasing to our Commander (II
Tim. 2:3, 4). We are to put on the armor of God, the
whole armor provided for us, to be ready for attack or
defense (Eph. 6:11-17). And the Christian, as John
Bunyan has pointed out in his *Pilgrim's Progress,* has
no armor for his back.

Failure in our own strength alone. Another lesson
taught us by the name *Jehovah-nissi* is that we cannot
wage this warfare in our own strength alone. When
Moses' arms grew weary the rod of God was lowered.
The enemy then prevailed and Israel was pressed back.
The lesson is quite clear. The rod was the symbol and
pledge of God's presence and power. Lowered, it could
not be seen. It was as though God were not present,
and therefore not in the mind of the people. They were
to learn that the evil forces of the world are powerful
and implacable, too great for man's own, unaided
strength. They could be strong only "by the hands of the
mighty God of Jacob" (Gen. 49:24). Moses learned
how indispensable God's presence was for victory and
success, but Israel forgot. When for their gross lack of
faith they were denied entrance into the Promised Land
at Kadesh-barnea, they repented, and were willing to
discard the evil report of the ten spies. When they at-

tempted the entrance into Canaan, they were told by Moses: "Go not up, for Jehovah is not among you." They perslsted, however, and were defeated and chased by the very Amalekites whom they had defeated at Rephidim (Num. 14:42-45). Israel suffered a similar defeat in its first encounter with the enemy in the Promised Land. (Jericho was not a battle in the sense of their active participation.) Because of sin God's presence was not with them at the battle of Ai. They went again alone and in their own strength, and were defeated. And God said: "Neither will I be with you any more, except ye destroy the accursed [thing] from among you" (Josh. 7:12). Nor in the work and warfare of our Christian experience can we do anything without Him who is not only the Jehovah of the Old Testament, but the Jesus of the New.

> Did we in our own strength confide,
>   Our striving would be losing;
> Were not the right Man on our side,
>   The Man of God's own choosing:
> Dost ask who that may be?
>   Christ Jesus it is He;
> Lord Sabaoth is His Name,
>   From age to age the same,
>   And He must win the battle.

We must be "strong in the Lord and in the power of his might." Then we may put on the whole armor of God and go confidently forth to wrestle with the enemy (Eph. 6:10-12).

The victory assured. The banner of Jehovah held aloft in Moses' upraised hand brought victory to His people. As they beheld that rod they must have been assured of victory. This is always assured to the people of God over the powers of evil and the enemy of our souls when His banner is over us. Before every battle of olden days the priest would approach the people in behalf of God and would say: "Hear, O Israel, ye approach this day unto battle against your enemies: let not your hearts faint, fear not, and do not tremble, neither be ye terrified because of them; for Jehovah your God is he that goeth with you, to fight for you against your enemies, to save you" (Deut. 20:3, 4). "The Lord is on my side; I will not fear what man can do unto me" (Ps. 118:6). The rod in Moses' hand, however, was only a symbol. Moses called the name of the altar which he built Jehovah-nissi—Jehovah, Himself, is my banner. Isaiah predicts a rod to come forth out of the stem of Jesse. This stem or root is also Himself to be an ensign, a banner of the peoples. That stem of Jesse is Christ, born of the seed of David according to the flesh (Rom. 1:3). He, therefore, is our banner, the banner of our redemption. When Moses lifted up a brazen serpent in the wilderness so that all who had been bitten by serpents might look and live, the word used for the pole on which he raised it is our word *banner*. The Lord Jesus said to Nicodemus: "And as Moses lifted up the serpent in the wilderness, even so must the Son of man be lifted up" (John 3:14). So the cross of Christ is our banner of God's mighty power in redemption. But He is also the banner of our warfare. He has conquered before us; "in the world ye shall have tribulation: but be of good cheer; I have overcome the world" (John 16:33). He, too, promises His presence. "Lo, I am with you all the days, even unto the end of the world" (Matt. 28:20). Faith in Him is the assurance of our victory, for "this

is the victory that overcometh the world, even our faith"
(I John 5:4). Our faith is in Him whom Paul tells us
has been placed "far above all principality, and power,
and might, and dominion, and every name that is
named" (Eph. 1:19-22), so that in Him we may successfully wrestle against those principalities and powers
of evil. "If God be for us, who can be against us?" For
"we are more than conquerors through him that loved
us" (Rom. 8:31, 37).

With Jehovah-Jesus, our banner, we may go from
strength to strength with each victory and we may say:
"Thanks be to God, which giveth us the victory through
our Lord Jesus Christ" (I Cor. 15:57), and "always
causeth us to triumph in Christ" (II Cor. 2:14).

> And tho' this world, with devils filled,
>   Should threaten to undo us;
> We will not fear, for God hath willed
>   His truth to triumph through us:
> The prince of darkness grim,—
>   We tremble not for him;
> His rage we can endure,
>   For lo! his doom is sure,
>   One little word shall fell him.

8

JEHOVAH-M'KADDESH

THE NAME *Jehovah-M'Kaddesh* is found in Leviticus
20:8. It means Jehovah who sanctifies. "Sanctify yourselves therefore, and be ye holy: for I am Jehovah your
God. . . . I am Jehovah which sanctify you" (Lev. 20:7,
8). Its appearance in the Book of Leviticus is most
appropriate. The order in which this name appears in
the revelations of the name *Jehovah,* and the particular
point of the people's experience when it was revealed
are most striking and suggestive. The order in which all
these names appear show purpose and progression, and
are evidently designed to meet the developing spiritual
life and need of the people.

Genesis, the book of beginnings, reveals the beginning
of sin. It therefore also reveals the provision of redemption from sin under the name of God, Jehovah-jireh—
God will provide. Exodus, as the book of redemption,
first exhibits the meaning of Jehovah-jireh in the Paschal
Lamb of redemption, by which Israel, Jehovah's people,
were redeemed from bondage in Egypt, which is the
type of our redemption from sin. In Exodus was also
revealed the name *Jehovah-rophe*, Jehovah who heals
life's wounds and sweetens its bitter experiences, as
signified by Israel's experience at Marah. Then came the
revelation of God as Jehovah-nissi at Rephidim, where

Amalek, the enemy, opposed and fought against Israel
—Jehovah, the banner over His people in that holy
warfare which all God's people must wage both within
themselves and without, in a hostile world.

Leviticus is the book of life, or walk and worship
of a people already redeemed. Therefore sanctification
is its most appropriate and important theme. It could
not appropriately be presented till redemption was fully
accomplished. It has been pointed out that the first mention of God as sanctifying is at the completion of Creation, when God sanctified the Sabbath day (Gen. 2:3).
But that day's rest was broken by the entrance of sin,
and its privilege lost. The word *sanctify* is not mentioned
again till in Exodus 13:1, 2 Jehovah commanded
Moses: "Sanctify unto me all the first-born . . . among
the children of Israel," the Israel of whom Jehovah had
already said, "Israel is my son, even my first-born"
(Exod. 4:22). The point is that only when redemption
from that sin which had broken the sanctification and
rest of the creation Sabbath had been accomplished,
even though only in type, could sanctification be re-
sumed. For Israel itself is evidently typical. As the first-
born in Israel were a figure of all Israel, and accepted
in behalf of all Israel, so Israel itself is typical as the
first-born among the nations for whom God will accomplish redemption. The Book of Leviticus therefore
sets forth that holy way in which a people already redeemed should walk worthy of their calling (Eph. 4:1),
and the spiritual worship which Jehovah demands of
them. Thus in connection with their moral and spiritual
purity this title of God is repeated six times in the two
chapters in Leviticus following its first appearance.

THE MEANING AND USE OF THE TERM "SANCTIFY"

The term *sanctify* occurs frequently in the Old Testament Scriptures. The Hebrew word which it translates is also translated by other English words such as *dedicate, consecrate, sanctuary, hallow,* and *holy,* but especially by the word *holy,* and often by *Holy One.* In its various forms it appears some 700 times. It has not been transferred or transliterated in our English Bibles as have other names studied, such as Jehovah-jireh, Jehovah-rophe, and Jehovah-nissi, and consequently it has often escaped attention as one of the compound names of Jehovah. Yet certainly there is no more important word in the Old Testament: nor does any other name more truly express the character of Jehovah and His requirements of His people than this name *Jehovah-M'Kaddesh* —Jehovah who sanctifies.

Its primary meaning, however, is to set apart or separate. This idea is most nearly rendered by the words *sanctify* or *hallow,* and the word *holy* stands for that which is hallowed or set apart. Whatever differences the various English renderings may suggest, the primary idea of separating or setting apart is common to them all.

As setting apart, the word is applied to times and seasons. God sanctified the Sabbath (Gen. 2:3; Exod. 20:8, 11), that is, He set it apart from other days. It was to be a different day. The great feasts and fasts of Israel with their deep spiritual and dispensational significance were times specially set apart and celebrated by holy convocations of the people (Lev. 23). That most wonderful of ancient Hebrew institutions, the year of Jubilee, coming after the seventh sabbaths of seven years, on the great Day of Atonement, ushered in with a great blowing of the trumpet, and proclaiming a new beginning of redemption and liberty for all, was also thus sanctified or specially set apart (Lev. 25:10).

The word *sanctify* in this sense was applied to places: the camp of Israel, the hill of Zion, the city of Jerusalem, the altar, the tabernacle, the Temple. The word so frequently used of both tabernacle and Temple is *mikdash*, so similar to this name of Jehovah, and meaning sanctuary. Thus it is a place set apart for the special presence and worship of Jehovah, who sanctifies. The Holy Land itself is thus a land set apart.

The word is again used in the setting apart of persons. Individuals were set apart from birth or even before birth. So Jeremiah was sanctified to Jehovah's service as a prophet to the nations (Jer. 1:5). The firstborn of Israel was set apart (Exod. 13:2). Upon the head of the high priest as the crowning mark of his high office was that perpetual sign of his setting apart to Jehovah: Holiness (*Kodesh*) to Jehovah (Evod. 28:36). And not only the priesthood but all the people were sanctified or set apart to Jehovah (Deut. 7:6).

The point involved in all these instances of the use of this word is contact with God. The Sabbath day was holy because God rested in it. The day was set apart by Israel as a pledge that God had sanctified this people to Himself (Exod. 31:13); and the mountain of the Lord of hosts was to be called the holy mount because Jehovah would dwell there (Zech. 8:3). The sanctuary itself was so named because it was the dwelling place of Jehovah among His people.

ITS APPLICATION TO JEHOVAH

This leads us to the second point of our discussion. As Himself the Holy One, Jehovah is apart from and above all else in the universe. "Jehovah he is God; there is none else beside him" (Deut. 4:35). "Thus saith Jehovah the King of Israel, and his redeemer Jehovah of hosts; I am the first, and I am the last; and beside me there is no God," says Isaiah (44:6); "a just God and a Saviour; there is none beside me" (Isa. 45:21). And I Samuel adds: "There is none holy as Jehovah: for there is none beside thee" (2:2). The most fundamental, the most solemn and impressive of all the attributes of the Deity is His holiness. John truly says, "God is love." But John is speaking here in a context which emphasizes the quality of love. And besides, that "love that God hath to us," of which John speaks, is that sacrificing, redeeming love of God, the very purpose of which is to make us fit for His holy presence. It is this holiness of which an old Scottish divine writes: "It is the balance . . . of all the attributes of Deity. Power without holiness would degenerate into cruelty; omniscience without holiness would become craft; justice without holiness would degenerate into revenge; and goodness without holiness would be passionate and intemperate fondness doing mischief rather than accomplishing good." It is this holiness which gives to God grandeur and majesty, and more than anything else constitutes His fullness and perfection.

Certainly it is the most important lesson about God in the Old Testament. In the key verse of the Book of Leviticus, which teaches how we may approach a holy God and walk in a manner approved of Him, it is writ-

ten, "For I Jehovah your God am holy." In the vision
that changed Isaiah's life and made him a great prophet,
there is that wonderful description of Jehovah, "Holy,
holy, holy is Jehovah of hosts" (Isa. 6:3). In the presence of that awful holiness, even the seraphim, creatures
of burning purity themselves, cover their eyes as if
afraid to behold or desecrate that holiness with their
gaze. Ever after, Jehovah is to Isaiah the Holy One of
Israel. This phrase is peculiar to Isaiah and occurs some
thirty times in his prophecy. The prophet Hosea also
speaks of Jehovah as "the Holy One in the midst of
thee" (11:9).

The Spirit of God is called the Holy Spirit. "Take
not thy holy spirit from me," pleads David (Ps. 51:11).
In a striking passage in which he speaks of Jehovah as
Israel's Saviour and also as the Angel of the Presence,
Isaiah also speaks of His Holy Spirit—truly a Trinity
(Isa. 63:8-11). "They rebelled, and vexed his holy
Spirit."

The holiness of God is especially made clear in contrast to the heathen deities, and the impurity and corruption of their nature and worship. It is because of this
that Israel is repeatedly and strongly urged: "Thou shalt
have no other gods before me" (Exod. 20:3). In contrast with them Jehovah is not corrupt in justice nor a
respecter of persons (Deut. 10:17). In fact, they are
really no gods, for the word *idol* in Psalm 96:5 and other
places is "a thing of nought." "Shall a man make gods
unto himself, and they are no gods?" says Jeremiah
(16:20). But they did sanctify to themselves gods, the
work of their own hands and the creatures of their imag-
inations. The gods of the heathen were a depraved lot,
caring only and busy about their own pleasures, lusts,

and quarrels. Cruel and unspeakable crimes were committed in their worship. "Their villainy upon earth gave them a title to a niche in the Pantheon of heathenism." Contrast the awful but beautiful holiness of God who is of purer eyes than to behold evil and cannot look upon iniquity (Hab. 1:13), holy and reverend is His name (Ps. 111:9; Luke 1:49).

It is in His transcendent holiness that the glory and beauty of Jehovah consist. In the great song of triumph sung by Moses and the children of Israel after their passage through the Red Sea (Exod. 15), which is also that song of Moses and of the Lamb sung by those who gain the victory over the beast and over his image (Rev. 15:3), the greatest tribute paid to Jehovah is in the words: "Who is like unto thee, O Jehovah . . . glorious in holiness." The cry of the seraphim, who veil their eyes in the presence of God's holiness, is "Holy, holy, holy, is the Lord of hosts": and then, "the whole earth is full of his glory." It is against the glory of God's holiness that all have sinned, for this is what Paul meant when he said: "All have sinned, and come short of the glory of God" (Rom. 3:23).

So also the beauty of the Lord is seen in His holiness. When the psalmist expresses the desire to behold the beauty of the Lord, it is in the house of the Lord, His Temple, the place of His holy presence that he expects to do so (Ps. 27:4). The beauty of the Lord is perfect. But beauty is a product of something, and the perfect beauty of the Lord is the product of His perfect holiness. A noted English preacher, J. D. Jones, has clearly illustrated this by calling attention to the fact that "the most striking feature in Swiss scenery, the glory and boast of Switzerland, is the vision of its mighty mountainpeaks clothed ever in their mantles of snowy white. Take the mountains away, and you have destroyed the beauty of Switzerland. And in much the same way you destroy the 'beauty of the Lord' if you forget His holiness. The basal thing in God's character is His 'awful purity.' We need to lift our eyes to these shining and snowclad peaks of the divine holiness if we are ever to be moved to say, 'How beautiful God is.' "

The Lord our God is holy—this was the first truth Israel learned about Jehovah. The law and the awe-inspiring circumstances connected with its giving on Mount Sinai were all intended to indelibly impress upon them this truth of the holiness of their Jehovah. It is this holiness of which, Moses reveals (Exod. 34:14), God is so jealous. His name is Jealous—that is, His holiness is pure and burning, and He cannot allow the worship of another in His people. "I will be sanctified in them that come nigh me," He declares (Lev. 10:3). His people are to sanctify Him in their hearts (Isa. 8:13), and to worship Him in the beauty of holiness (I Chron. 16:29; Ps. 29:2).

ITS APPLICATION TO GOD'S PEOPLE

It is the glory and beauty of His holiness that God wishes to impart. It is no idle prayer the psalmist utters when he says: "Let the beauty of Jehovah our God be upon us" (Ps. 90:17). It is a God-implanted desire, and it finds its answer in the words of Peter that we are made "partakers of the divine nature" through great and precious promises made to us (II Peter 1:4). It is God's desire that the man whom He made in His own image, who corrupted that image through sin, should be restored to that image which is "righteousness and true holiness," putting on that new man which is after God (Eph. 4:24).

When God began a new experiment, so to speak, in His purpose for man's redemption by first selecting a people, He set them apart or sanctified them to that purpose saying: "Speak unto the congregation of the children of Israel, and say unto them, Ye shall be holy: for I Jehovah your God am holy" (Lev. 19:2). A holy God demands holiness in His people. A God separate from all that is evil, too pure to behold evil, the very antithesis of all evil, requires that the people He chooses be also separate from all evil and separated to the purpose for which He chose them. Hence the emphatic command, first of all, that they serve no other gods but Himself, for a people become like the gods they serve. This is abundantly demonstrated in Israel's history.

Then again this people was to be apart, separated from all the peoples round about them in order to avoid the contagion of their corruption. All the institutions of ancient Israel's economy, its whole social and spiritual structure, its ceremonies and rites, the prohibition of certain foods and of intermarriage were designed to insulate them for a while from the rest of mankind, and to make them the best possible instrument for God's purpose. Perhaps it was also, as one writer has suggested, to show them even under the best circumstances and surroundings, that fallen man's "heart is deceitful above all things and desperately wicked"; that his defilement is from within himself also; that there is no hope of redemption and holiness apart from God. "Ye shall be holy for I Jehovah your God am holy" was the magnificent ideal placed before Israel. To be God's peculiar

treasure and the instrument of His holy purpose was
Israel's grand destiny. Jehovah Himself was the model
of separateness, of holiness, ever before them in striv-
ing after this destiny.

The term *sanctified* or *separated,* however, means
more than position or relationship in regard to Jehovah.
It means participation in the nature of Jehovah, His
character and works. It is not without grounds that the
word *holy,* although primarily meaning set apart, has
come to represent moral and spiritual qualities. To be
separate and apart from all evil and wickedness is not
merely to be negative but to be good. They were commanded not only not to do "after the doings of the land
of Egypt, wherein ye dwelt . . . and after the doings of
the land of Canaan, whither I bring you . . ." but "ye
shall do my judgments, and keep my ordinances, to walk
therein" (Lev. 18:3, 4). Holiness is also positive and
active. The people of God, therefore, must be holy in
practice as well as separated in position. The one is
meaningless without the other. This sanctifying or separating of His people is, on the part of Jehovah, an act;
but the practice of holiness in His people is the working
out of that act for themselves. "I am Jehovah which
sanctify you," but we read in the preceding verse, "Sanctify yourselves therefore, and be ye holy" (Lev. 20:7).
God has endowed us with free will. He recognizes that
prerogative of free will. He commands His people to be
holy but He will not force them to be so. He placed within Israel, on the basis of redemption, the power to be
holy, and provided them with every incentive to holiness, but man must of his own free will exercise that
provision and power. Jehovah would have man's free
and willing separation and holiness, otherwise it is no

holiness at all, for without free will it loses its moral character. Therefore this holiness is a process, not an act accomplished once for all. It lasts as long as man shall live and calls for his continued exercise and choice. This exercise was to make for growth in the holiness that a holy God required of a separated people.

Jehovah, as apart from and above all creatures, as sanctified and holy, is immeasurably transcendent; but as the Sanctifier of His people, setting them apart to Himself and His purpose, He becomes immanent, indwelling and empowering them by His Holy Spirit to live holy and acceptably before Him.

What Jehovah was to His people in the Old Testament, as Jehovah the Holy One who sanctifies, the Lord Jesus Christ is in the New Testament.

As to Himself, He was from His very conception and birth the Son of God and the holy child born to the Virgin Mary by the power of the Holy Spirit (Luke 1:35). As the only begotten of the Father, the brightness of His glory, and the express image of His person, He perfectly manifested the glory and beauty of the Father. This, it was shown, is chiefly expressed by the perfect holiness of Jehovah. So the Lord Jesus, the Jehovah-Jesus, was altogether holy and spotless in His life. He was "in all points tempted like as we are, yet without sin" (Heb. 4:15). In contrast to the Aaronic high priesthood, He became our High Priest "who is holy, harmless, undefiled, separate from sinners, and made higher than the heavens" (Heb. 7:26). He was made sin for us, in His redeeming love, but He Himself knew no sin (II Cor. 5:21).

He set Himself wholly apart as the Son and manifestation of the Father to do the Father's will, and surrendered Himself completely to it. "Lo, I come, as it is written in the volume of the book, to do thy will, O God" (Heb. 10:7-9). He became our Sanctification as Paul says (I Cor. 1:30). "We are sanctified through the offering of the body of Jesus Christ once for all" (Heb. 10:10), and by this offering "he hath perfected forever them that are sanctified" (Heb. 10:14).

What Israel was meant to be nationally we also are to be as a Church and personally. Peter quotes the very words of Leviticus in urging this. "But as he which hath called you is holy, so be ye holy in all manner of conversation [or living, as the A.S.V. more clearly puts it]; because it is written, Be ye holy; for I am holy" (I Peter 1:15, 16). For we are, he continues, "a chosen generation, a royal priesthood, an holy nation, a peculiar people; that ye should show forth the excellencies of him who hath called you out of darkness into his marvelous light" (2:9).

To such holiness, or separateness, we have been elected. "The God and Father of our Lord Jesus Christ" has "chosen us in him before the foundation of the world, that we should be holy and without blame before him in love" (Eph. 1:4). We are called with a holy calling (II Tim. 1:9).

As in the Old Testament, so in the New, we are set apart or sanctified on the basis of our redemption in Christ. "Who hath saved us, and called us with an holy calling" (II Tim. 1:9). "We are sanctified through the offering of the body of Jesus Christ once for all" (Heb. 10:10). "That he might sanctify the people with his own blood," he "suffered without the gate" (Heb. 13:12).

This sanctification or separateness of life is accomplished by the Word of His truth: "Sanctify them through thy truth: thy word is truth," said the Lord Jesus in His great prayer (John 17:17), for they were not of the world even as He was not of the world (v. 16). He is our example in this: "For their sakes I sanctify myself, that they also might be sanctified through the truth" (v. 19). But He has also empowered us to this through the Holy Spirit, who is the Spirit of holiness and power. He is the Author of this our holiness, who makes our bodies the temples of His presence and produces the fruit of the Spirit, the love, joy, peace, goodness, faith, etc., of which Paul speaks in Galatians 5:22, 23.

Here we are reminded of the truth that, as in the Old Testament sanctification was not only with regard to our position in Jehovah, but with regard also to life and practice, so also in the New Testament; for after speaking of the fruit of the Holy Spirit in a believer, Paul continues: "If we live in the Spirit, let us also walk in the Spirit" (Gal. 5:25). And if we walk in the Spirit we shall not fulfill the lusts of the flesh.

Again and again we are exhorted to sanctification of life. Our bodies are to be presented a living sacrifice, holy to God and acceptable (Rom. 12:1, 2). Contrasting their former mode of life, Paul addressed the Corinthians: "Such were some of you: but ye are washed, but ye are sanctified . . . in the name of the Lord Jesus, and by the Spirit of our God" (I Cor. 6:11). Our new man is created in righteousness and true holiness (Eph. 4:24). We are Christ's workmanship created in Him unto good works in which we are to walk (Eph. 2:10), and which we are to maintain (Titus 3:8).

The chastenings of the Lord also are to this end, that

we might be partakers of His holiness, that "holiness, without which no man shall see the Lord" (Heb. 12:10, 14). Only the pure in heart can see God.

It is the Church's glorious destiny to be presented holy and spotless to her Lord, a glorious Church. And in what does this glory consist? It is in "not having spot, or wrinkle, or any such thing; but that it should be holy and without blemish" (Eph. 5:26, 27); and that we shall be like Him when He shall appear. "And every man that hath this hope in him purifieth himself, even as he is pure" (I John 3:3).

"For this is the will of God, even your sanctification" (I Thess. 4:3), the sanctification of the whole spirit and soul and body blameless unto the coming of our Lord Jesus Christ (I Thess. 5:23).

9

JEHOVAH-SHALOM

THE NAME *Jehovah-shalom* is found in Judges 6:24: "Then Gideon built an altar unto Jehovah and called it Jehovah-shalom," which means Jehovah is peace.

THE OCCASION OF ITS REVELATION

It was more than 200 years since Jehovah had revealed Himself to His people as Jehovah-M'Kaddesh, Jehovah who sanctifies. Joshua had long since died. The land had been conquered and divided among the tribes, but nothing approaching national unity had been achieved in all this time. There was no central government or worship. It was a period in which "every man did that which was right in his own eyes."

For after Joshua died Israel began to forget Jehovah their God, and to turn to the gods of the peoples round about. A new generation arose which forgot Him who, as Jehovah-jireh, had provided redemption from bondage in Egypt through the blood of the Paschal Lamb, and with great and mighty wonders had led them out. They were no longer mindful of Him who, as Jehovah-rophe, had healed their sicknesses and sorrows, and would have prevented such misfortunes from coming upon them. They suffered defeats because they turned their backs upon Him who, as Jehovah-nissi, had been their banner of victory in trial and struggle. They would not sanctify themselves to Him who, as Jehovah-M'Kaddesh, had sanctified them to His cause, but they corrupted themselves with idolatries and their abominations. Thus they lost their purity, peace, prosperity, and liberty.

Israel could not appear to realize its destiny as a special and separate people, set apart to Jehovah's service and purpose in the midst of the nations. They seemed unable to rise above a material conception and plane of living. To live, to multiply, to inherit the land—this seemed to them a sufficient fulfillment of their function, an error common to this very day. It is not difficult to understand, then, the attraction of the grossly materialistic gods of the heathen for them.

Without a sense of mission there was no common purpose of uniting as one people. Without spiritual vision they fell an easy prey to the appetites and lusts of the flesh. Every apostasy brought punishment and misery—a chastening of Jehovah to awaken them to their spiritual calling. Repentance brought deliverance through the leadership of judges raised up of God. Every succeeding apostasy called for even severer chastening by means of the surrounding nations—chastenings which not only deprived them of the fruits of their land and labors, but brought them into slavery. Without obedience to Jehovah they had no right to the land. His people must be more than mere tillers of the soil and dressers of vineyards (in any age); otherwise they should not enjoy the land. They tilled and planted, but they did not reap. As Jehovah had sown spiritual seed in their hearts, and they had allowed their idolatrous neighbors to trample and tear it out by the imitation of their corrupt idolatries, so now these same heathen embittered and endangered Israel's physical existence. The enemy they should have completely subdued, subdued them, sweeping over the land, reaping what Israel had sown, and driving them into the caves and rocks. Israel was compelled to make underground caves with air holes, like the catacombs, to which they could flee at the enemy's approach, with watchmen constantly posted to warn them of it.

It was a period of alternating prosperity and adversity, of sinning and repenting, of slavery and deliverance. They would grievously sin and be brought very low. In their extremity they would remember Jehovah their God and cry out to Him for deliverance. Jehovah would hear them and raise up a deliverer for them. Then after serving Jehovah, Israel would fall away again, and the whole process would be repeated.

Gideon was a young man in a time of severe oppression by the Midianites. Israel did evil in the sight of the Lord, and He delivered them into the hand of the Midianites seven years. They were compelled to live in dens in the mountains. Midian and her allies, including the Amalekites, would come with great hordes of men and of cattle and eat up the land, destroying what they could not devour and leaving neither sustenance, nor implements, nor animals. Gideon was threshing a little wheat, saved somehow from the all-devouring hordes of the enemy, and in the secrecy of the wine-press, for fear of them, when the angel of Jehovah appeared to him with a promise of deliverance in response to Israel's cry. Gideon, after some doubt, hesitation, and reassurance, accepted the promise and the challenge. In faith he reared an altar which he called Jehovah-shalom, in confident anticipation of victory and peace.

MEANING AND USE OF THE WORD "SHALOM"

This word is one of the most significant in the Old Testament, its various shades of meaning harmonizing with the doctrine of the atonement as the basis of peace with God.

It is translated sometimes as "whole," as in Deuteronomy 27:6: "Thou shalt build the altar of Jehovah thy God of whole stones." As "finished" the same word is used in Daniel 5:26: "God hath numbered thy kingdom, and finished it." So Solomon "finished" the temple (I Kings 9:25). As "full" it is used in Genesis 15:16: "The iniquity of the Amorites is not yet full." It is used in the sense of making good a loss and is translated as "make good" in Exodus 21:34; 22:5, 6, and in other similar passages in the laws of Israel relating to losses inflicted by carelessness. Thus also it is translated as restitution or repay. In the physical and material sense of wholeness or completeness it is translated as "welfare" and "well." In Genesis 43:27 Joseph inquires concerning the welfare of his brothers, and using the same word again in the same verse asks if their father is well. So Joab in II Samuel 20:9, before dealing the treacherous and fatal blow, asks Amasa, "Art thou in health, my brother?" It is quite frequently used as "render" and "pay" or "perform" in the sense of fulfilling or completing obligations. This is particularly true of vows rendered to the Lord. "Pay thy vows unto the most High," says the psalmist (50:14). "When thou shalt vow a vow unto Jehovah thy God, thou shalt not be slack to pay it: for Jehovah thy God will surely require it of thee; and it would be sin in thee" (Deut. 23:21). On the contrary, "the wicked borroweth and payeth not again" (Ps. 37:21). It is translated "requite" and "recompense" in a few instances. As the One who deals justly and makes right, Jehovah says in Deuteronomy 32:35, "To me belongeth vengeance, and recompense [*shillem*]." About twenty times it is translated "perfect." "Give unto Solomon my son a perfect heart," David asks of Jehovah (I Chron. 29:19). And Solomon echoes this in his own exhortation to the people when the house of the Lord was perfected (*shalem*): "Let your heart therefore be perfect [*shalem*] with Jehovah our God" (I Kings 8:61); that is, let it be in wholeness or in harmony with God. And this is the basic idea underlying all the various translations of this one Hebrew word—a harmony of relationship or a reconciliation based upon the completion of a transaction, the payment of a debt, the giving of satisfaction. Therefore this word is most often and most appropriately translated "peace" some 170 times. It expressed the deepest desire and need of the human heart. It represented the greatest measure of contentment and satisfaction in life. Of King Solomon it was said that in his reign Judah and Israel dwelt safely (that is, in confidence and peace), every man under his vine and under his fig tree (I Kings 4:25). It was to be characteristic of the reign of Messiah, the righteous Branch of David, of whom Solomon was typical, that Judah and Israel should dwell safely— in peace (Jer. 23:6). One of the great names of Messiah was to be "Prince of Peace" (Isa. 9:6), and Jerusalem, Messiah's city, means city of peace or possession of peace. Peace was the most common form of greeting as it is to this day in Bible and even other lands.

Finally, it is also, obviously, the word used in "peace offering." The peace offering was one of the blood sacrifices of which the shed blood was the atonement on which reconciliation and peace were based (Lev. 3; 7:11-21). In the peace offering this restoration of fellowship between God and man, broken by sin, but now atoned for by the shed blood, was indicated by the fact that both God and man, priest and people, partook of the offering.

The various shades of meaning contained in this word all indicate that every blessing, temporal and spiritual, is included in restoring man to that peace with God which was lost by the fall.

JEHOVAH, THE SOURCE OF PEACE

Jehovah in His own person is perfect peace. This He must be if He is to be the source of peace to mankind. He is grieved at the sin and corruption of the world, which at creation He had pronounced so good. He is stirred to wrath at the evil of the wicked. He is not indifferent to the sorrows and needs of the race as well as of His people. "I have surely seen the affliction of my people . . . I know their sorrow" (Exod. 3:7); and Isaiah tells us, "In all their affliction he was afflicted" (63:9). In the Book of Judges, when, after Gideon's time, Israel had again fallen into sin, we read in 10:16 that "his soul was grieved for the misery of Israel." Yet none of these things disturb His peace in the sense that they can destroy or unsteady the perfect balance of His divine nature. He could never give to others a peace that passes understanding if He were not perfect, unfailing peace Himself. This is our hope and assurance.

But He is the source of peace in His attitude toward us. "For I know the thoughts that I think toward you, saith Jehovah, thoughts of peace, and not of evil" (Jer. 29:11). And through Isaiah He speaks to His people: "O that thou hadst hearkened to my commandments! Then had thy peace been like a river, and thy righteousness as the waves of the sea" (48:18). Nothing is more clearly indicated in the Scriptures than that His desires toward all mankind and especially toward His people are desires of good. He has no pleasure in the death of the wicked but only that he turn from his evil way and live (Ezek. 33:11). To this end the Scriptures are full of the promise and purpose of peace. "If ye walk in my statutes . . . and do them . . . I will give peace in the land, and ye shall lie down, and none shall make you afraid: and I will rid evil beasts out of the land, neither shall the sword go through your land" (Lev. 26:3, 6). "The Lord will bless his people with peace," says David (Ps. 29:11). "Lord, thou wilt ordain peace for us," says Isaiah (26:12). Speaking of a future glory of Jerusalem Isaiah continues: "For thus saith Jehovah, Behold, I will extend peace to her like a river" (66:12). And it forms the apex of the great high priestly benediction of the triune Jehovah, with which Aaron and his sons were commanded to bless the children of Israel: "Jehovah lift up his countenance upon thee, and give thee peace" (Num. 6:24-26).

THE PRESENCE OF JEHOVAH IS PEACE

It was Jehovah Himself who appeared to Gideon, in contrast to the prophet who had first been sent to the people. For the angel of Jehovah of Judges 6:22 is addressed by Gideon in the same verse as "O Jehovah Elohim," and in the next verse He is spoken of as the Jehovah who spoke peace to Gideon. This was the most striking manifestation of Jehovah yet made in all this chaotic, restless, struggling period of Israel's history. Of Othniel it was stated that the spirit of Jehovah came upon him (3:10). The Lord raised up Ehud, another judge (3:15). Barak is called through the prophetess and judge Deborah (4:6). But Gideon appears to begin a second period in the history of the Judges. A new and more striking manifestation of Jehovah appears necessary if the people are to be arrested in the evil course which seemed to be hastening toward a final crisis. Thus Jehovah appears Himself to Gideon, and the remaining and larger portion of the book, though covering little more than a century, exhibits God's dealings with His people in much fuller detail than the first few chapters which cover about two centuries.

As in the Book of Leviticus Jehovah was most appropriately revealed as Jehovah-M'Kaddesh, Jehovah who sanctifies, so the revelation Jehovah-shalom, Jehovah is peace, appears most appropriately and opportunely in the Book of Judges. After the conquest of Canaan, Israel should have entered into its rest, typical of that rest spoken of in Hebrews 4. It was of this rest in Canaan that Moses spoke in the wilderness when he said: "Ye are not as yet come to the rest and to the inheritance, which Jehovah your God giveth you" (Deut. 12:9). And the following verse speaks of that rest as "over Jordan." But because of disobedience Israel failed to gain even that typical rest. Nothing is more characteristic of the Book of Judges than its chaotic restlessness. Over and over again after deliverance from bondage and misery, we read that the land had rest for awhile. Insecurity and fear had never been greater than in Gideon's day.

Thus it is that the angel of Jehovah comes to Gideon saying, "Jehovah is with thee" (Judges 6:12). Israel knew no peace because it no longer knew God's presence. This is the answer to Gideon's question: "O my Lord, If Jehovah be with us, why then is all this befallen us?" Jehovah was not with Israel. He is with those who are with Him. The word of the prophet to a king of Judah was: "Jehovah is with you, while ye be with him; and if ye seek him, he will be found of you; but if ye forsake him, he will forsake you" (II Chron. 15:2). There is never peace to the wicked. "The wicked are like the troubled sea, when it cannot rest, whose waters cast up dirt and mire. There is no peace, saith my God, to the wicked" (Isa. 57:20, 21). The root idea of the word translated "wicked" is restlessness. They do not know the way of peace, continues the prophet, and whoever walks in their way doesn't know peace (59:7, 8).

When Gideon realized the character of the visitor, he was afraid (Judges 6:22). Perhaps his doubt and hesitancy to believe the promise of deliverance made him fear. But evidently it was the consciousness of human sinfulness in the presence of the Divine. Man knows that all is not well, or whole, or peace between God and himself. Man needs to be reconciled to God, but reconciliation can be effected only by paying the price of sin. But the price of sin is death. How then can God save the sinner in that case? In the Old Testament, as we know, it was by the temporary, typical expedient of an animal substitute whose shed blood paid the price, restored harmony, and brought peace.

At the angel's command Gideon had laid such an offering on an altar of rock nearby. As a token of acceptance the angel had caused fire to come up out of the rock to consume the offering. On the basis of this the angel now says to Gideon: "Peace be unto thee; fear not: thou shalt not die" (Judges 6:23). Then Gideon built the altar which he called Jehovah-shalom. The experience in the presence of the angel of Jehovah had no doubt taught him also that Jehovah who sanctifies His people and demands a sanctification and purity of life on their part will enable them to fulfill His demands upon them if they will yield themselves to Him. Man, conscious of his sinfulness, naturally shrinks from God's holiness and realizes the impossibility of being in himself what a holy God requires, but God reassures us and speaks peace to our hearts by saying: "I am Jehovah who doth sanctify you and enables you to live in my presence and fellowship." This is assured in the title *Jehovah-shalom*. There is perfect peace to those who know Jehovah as Jehovah-M'Kaddesh, Jehovah who sanctifies, and are sanctified, separated, holy to Him. How beautifully the prophet Isaiah expresses this! "Open ye the gates, that the righteous nation which keepeth the truth may enter in. Thou wilt keep him in perfect peace, whose mind is stayed on thee . . ." (Isa. 26:2-4).

Gideon now believed that even though his family was small, with Jehovah one could chase a thousand, and two put ten thousand to flight. The altar he erected was not for sacrifice, but a memorial and witness testifying to the fact that Jehovah desires certainly not the destruction but the peace of those He has already saved and set apart for His service; that in this service of His He bestows every requirement and meets every need—of sanctification, steadfastness, wisdom, courage, boldness, and victory.

JEHOVAH-JESUS, THE FULLNESS AND PERFECTION OF OUR PEACE

Gideon's name for Jehovah finds its fullest expression and realization in the New Testament. It is frequently applied to God, who is called "the God of peace" (Rom. 15:33; II Cor. 13:11; Heb. 13:20, etc.). It is also applied indirectly to the Lord Jesus Christ.

He also in His own person is perfect peace. He speaks of "my peace" as when in John 14:27 He says to His disciples: "My peace I give unto you," and, "These things have I spoken unto you, that in me ye might have peace" (John 16:33). As with Jehovah in the Old Testament, He also was touched with the feeling of our infirmities. He Himself suffered being tempted. As was predicted of Him, He bore our griefs and carried our sorrows (Isa. 53:4). Nevertheless He carried within Himself that perfect repose of spirit which belongs to God alone, and which alone could say to others: "Come unto me, all ye that labor, and are heavy laden, and I will give you rest . . . rest unto your souls" (Matt. 11:28, 29). It was an evidence of His deity.

He is the Prince of Peace promised in the Old Testament (Isa. 9:6). Before His birth Zacharias announced Him as the day-spring from on high who had visited His people "to guide our feet into the way of peace" (Luke 1:78, 79), while at His birth a multitude of the heavenly host sang "peace on earth" (Luke 2:14).

He also preached and promised peace. How often He

said to those He healed and comforted, "Go in peace!" How He wept over Jerusalem which would reject Him, saying: "If thou hadst known . . . the things which belong to thy peace" (Luke 19:42). His first words to His disciples after rising from the dead are, "Peace be unto you." The burden of Peter's first message to the Gentiles was the preaching of "peace by Jesus Christ" (Acts 10:36), who, says Paul, "came and preached peace to you which were afar off, and to them that were nigh" (Eph. 2:17).

He accomplished that peace for us. "Being justified by faith, we have peace with God through our Lord Jesus Christ" (Rom. 5:1). It is through His death that we were reconciled to God (Rom. 5:10), for "God was in Christ, reconciling the world unto himself" (II Cor. 5:19); "having made peace," continues Paul, "through the blood of his cross, by him to reconcile all things unto himself; by him, I say, whether they be things in earth, or things in heaven" (Col. 1:20). By His own precious blood He broke down the barrier of sin that stood between us and God and opened for us that new and living way into the holiest of all. And we who believe in the Lord Jesus Christ may enter there with boldness in the full assurance of a perfect reconciliation and peace.

But the measure of our sanctification to Him and our continued trust in Him is the measure of our peace in Him. "The peace of God, which passeth all understanding, shall keep your hearts and minds through Christ Jesus," says the apostle (Phil. 4:7), but he suggests in verse 6 that it depends on the measure of our trust, and in verse 9 on the measure of our obedience. In Colossians 3:15 he tells us we are to let the peace of God rule in our hearts. For to be spiritually minded is peace (Rom. 8:6), and many believers are more or less carnally minded, which is to lack that peace. Peace is one of the fruits of that spirit which is the Holy Spirit, the Spirit of sanctification. And Paul prays that the God of peace Himself sanctify us wholly that (in His peace) our spirit, soul, and body be preserved entire, without blame at the coming of our Lord Jesus Christ (I Thess. 5:23, A.S.V.).

Through Him we have peace with God. He is to us the peace of God. There is no hope of peace apart from Him either for individuals or nations. First righteousness, then peace. To this both Old and New Testaments bear witness. "The work of righteousness shall be peace;" says Isaiah, "and the effect of righteousness quietness and assurance forever" (32:17). But the only righteousness acceptable to God is the righteousness of the Lord Jesus Christ and those upon whom He bestows it through their faith in Him. Those who are not thus righteous do not know the way of peace (Rom. 3:11, 17). That mysterious type of Christ, Melchizedek, is first king of righteousness, and after that king of Salem or peace (Heb. 7:2). It is glory to God in the highest, and then and then only, peace on earth, good will among men (Luke 2:14). Peace is everywhere spoken of in the New Testament as from God the Father and from the Lord Jesus Christ. It may be had only by reconciliation with God through the blood of Christ who is the Jehovah-shalom of the New Testament.

10

JEHOVAH-TSIDKENU

THE NAME *Jehovah-Tsidkenu* means Jehovah our righteousness. It appears in Jeremiah's prophecy of a "righteous Branch" and a "King" who is to appear; "and this is his name whereby he shall be called, Jehovah our Righteousness" (Jer. 23:5, 6).

THE OCCASION OF THE PROPHECY

When Jeremiah uttered this prophecy, the kingdom of Judah was hastening to its fall. More than a hundred years before, the ten tribes of the kingdom of Israel had been taken captive never to return. But apparently Judah had learned nothing from this lesson, and it sinned perhaps even more grievously than its sister kingdom in the north. Jeremiah's ministry began during the reign of the good king Josiah. Till this time good kings and bad kings, reformations and counterreformations had succeeded each other, a sad reflection upon the unstable spiritual condition of the people and their rulers, and revealing a downward moral and spiritual trend which could only end in disaster. The history of the period of the Judges appears to repeat itself here. Jehovah in His goodness and patience raised up pious and devout kings to succeed unrighteous, wicked kings, but it failed to arrest their downward trend.

The good king Josiah, who had followed the particularly wicked and cruel Manasseh and Amon, instituted sweeping reforms and a great spiritual revival which were brought to an abrupt end by his unfortunate and untimely death. His successors swept them all away. Their doings may be summed up in that familiar formula, which might well have served as an epitaph for them all—"he did evil in the sight of Jehovah." Conditions went from bad to worse spiritually, morally, materially. Even the priests, as well as the princes and people, polluted the very house of the Lord in Jerusalem, practicing every abomination of the heathen round about (Ezek. 8). The land was full of oppression and violence, political intrigue and unrest. Jehovah's warnings went unheeded; His messengers the prophets were mocked and despised and misused "until the wrath of the Lord arose against his people, till there was no remedy" (II Chron. 36:16). Even at the time of Josiah's death it was already too late, for "the Lord turned not from the fierceness of his great wrath, wherewith his anger was kindled against Judah, because of all the provocations that Manasseh had provoked him withal. And the Lord said, "I will remove Judah also out of my sight, as I have removed Israel, and will cast off this city of Jerusalem which I have chosen, and the house of which I said, My name shall be there" (II Kings 23:26, 27). Judah's day of grace had already expired.

Jeremiah predicted the captivity of Judah and counseled submission to Babylon, the instrument of Jehovah's judgment against Judah. But would not this mean the defeat of God's own purpose and promise! Had He not promised to establish David's kingdom and throne forever (II Sam. 7:16, 17)! Jehovah had promised that, and He would keep the promise that there should never fail David a man to sit upon his throne (I Kings 2:4), even though it was to be fulfilled only on condition that David's descendants would walk before Jehovah "in truth with all their heart and with all their soul." For Jeremiah predicted not only that Israel would return from captivity and be restored to its land, but that Jehovah would raise up to David a Righteous Branch, a King who should reign and prosper and do judgment and justice in the earth, and bring peace and security to Israel, and who should be called Jehovah our Righteousness.

There is a striking and significant similarity between the name of this Righteous Branch and King of Jeremiah's prophecy and the name of Judah's last king— "Zedekiah," which means the righteousness of Jehovah. His name had originally been *Mattaniah,* which means the gift of Jehovah. Strange to say, his name had been changed to Zedekiah by the king of Babylon. Was it a scathing rebuke by Nebuchadnezzar of Judah's defection from its God? Perhaps it was intended to vindicate the justice and righteousness of Jehovah in all that had befallen this people, and the judgment about to fall upon them. Perhaps it was a reminder of what might have been. For Israel had steadily and determinedly trod the downward path of retrogression from its God, occasionally, through Jehovah's mercy, halting and retracing a few steps, only to turn back again. "They have turned unto me the back, and not the face" (Jer. 32:33). They despised His provision of redemption as Jehovah-jireh. Consequently He could not be to them Jehovah-rophe, who heals. They were a people, as Isaiah says, without soundness from the sole of the foot to the crown of the

head, full of open wounds, bruises, and putrefying sores
(Isa. 1:6). Without Jehovah-nissi, their banner, they
were defeated at every turn. Refusing to sanctify themselves to Jehovah-M'Kaddesh, their sanctifier, they became corrupt and degenerate. Ezekiel sees their elders
in the very Temple worshiping creeping things and
abominable beasts (Ezek. 8:10, 11). Forsaking Jehovah-shalom, their peace, they were torn by internal dis-
sension and violence, and subjected by outward aggres-
sion and conquest.

It must have been in the reign of Zedekiah that the
great prophecy of Jehovah-tsidkenu was given. Certainly the prophecy of Jeremiah 33:16, which speaks of
Jerusalem as Jehovah-tsidkenu, because of the presence
there of Jehovah-tsidkenu, was made in Zedekiah's
reign. And what a striking contrast is here presented!
All that Judah's kings should have been as representa-
tives of Jehovah, at least typically, and as summed up
in the name of Judah's last king, Zedekiah (the righteousness of Jehovah), this Righteous Branch, and King
of David's line, would be. And in Him, as Jeremiah declares in 33:6-26, Judah would be once more redeemed,
healed, cleansed, victorious, at peace and made righteous. For the nature of His kingdom was to be spiritual
rather than political and its chief characteristic righteousness, which was to be not of themselves but of that
King who should be Jehovah.

MEANING AND USE OF THE TERM "TSEDEK"

The word *tsidkenu* is derived from *tsedek*—righteousness. It meant originally to be stiff or straight. There is
certainly no more significant word in the Old Testa-

ment. The Hebrew word cannot be adequately translated by any one English word. It signifies God's dealings with men under the ideas of righteousness, justification, and acquittal.

It is applied to the outward obligations and relationships of men. The Book of Leviticus, where Jehovah is revealed as M'Kaddesh who sanctifies and demands sanctification of life, the book which reveals the basis of approach and manner of worship, also reveals the standards of right and just relationships among men. "Ye shall do no unrighteousness in judgment . . . in weight, or in measure. Just balances, just weights . . . shall ye have: I am Jehovah your God . . ." (Lev. 19:35, 36). In Deuteronomy 25:15 such a righteous practice is one of the conditions of prosperity and stay in their land.

Among the ancient Romans justice was represented by a person with a pair of balanced scales in her hand. Thus Job pleads: "Let me be weighed in an even balance," or balance of righteousness, "that God may know mine integrity" (31:6). The psalmist pictures all men, both high and low, as going up when laid on the balances (62:9). It is a coming short in the righteous practices which men owe God even in their relationships toward one another.

Modern orthodox Jewry still conceives of God as weighing their good deeds over against the bad. On new year's day the process begins and on the Day of Atonement it ends and judgment is sealed for the year. The ten days in between are spent in a desperate effort by charity, prayer, and fasting to tip the balances in one's favor, although there is never certainty as to which way it may have gone.

The word *tsedek* is also used of a full weight or measure toward God in the spiritual sense. Thus Israel was commanded to walk in the paths of righteousness and to offer the sacrifices of righteousness, putting their trust in the Lord (Ps. 4:5). These sacrifices are described also as a broken spirit and a contrite heart (Ps. 51:17), because of failure to measure up to such a full standard of righteousness; for as Job says: "How shall a man be righteous with God?" (9:2).

It is used in the sense of rendering justice and making right. The judges and officers of Israel were to judge the people with righteous judgment (Deut. 16:18). They were especially warned against perverting righteous judgment, but they justify or make righteous the wicked for a reward, says Isaiah (5:23). They decree unrighteous decrees (10:1). Isaiah pictures Jehovah as looking for righteousness in judgment, but finding the cry of the oppressed (5:7).

The word is used hundreds of times in the Scriptures both as right, righteous, righteousness, and also as just, justify, declare innocent. Human language is at best insufficient to convey the full comprehension of the ideas of righteousness and justification contained in this word. It is only as we see it exhibited in God's character and acts that we see it clearly.

JEHOVAH THE SOURCE OF RIGHTEOUSNESS

Jehovah is Himself perfect righteousness; He is the perfectly righteous One. Jehovah is a *Tsadik*—a righteous One, says the psalmist (129:4). As an *El-Tsadik* —a righteous God, there is none to compare with Him, says Isaiah (45:21). He is the Rock whose work is per-

fect, all of whose ways are justice. *Tsadik*—righteous
and right is He (Deut. 32:4). His righteousness is an
everlasting righteousness and His testimonies are righteous forever (Ps. 119:142, 144). Righteousness and
justice are the very foundations of His throne (Ps.
89:14; 97:2). Therefore in all His dealings He is righteous.

In contrast to Jehovah's perfect righteousness is man's
lack of righteousness and the evil of his ways. The constant testimony of Scripture is to this effect. "What is
man that he should be clean? And he which is born of
woman, that he should be righteous?" asks Eliphaz of
Job (15:14). The psalmist represents Jehovah as looking in vain from heaven upon the children of men to
see if there be any that understand and do good. And
the verdict is: "There is none that doeth good, no, not
one" (Ps. 14:3). The apostle Paul, quoting this very
passage in the New Testament, says, "There is none
righteous, no, not one" (Rom. 3:20), and he concludes
that "all have sinned, and come short of the glory of
God" (Rom. 3:23).

Israel is sharply reminded that not because it has any
righteousness of its own does Jehovah give them the
land to possess. On the contrary, they are a stiffnecked
and sinful people. It is only because He would perform
His promise to the fathers and carry out His purpose
that they inherit the land (Deut. 9:4-6). The prophet
Isaiah regards as filthy rags what he had once considered
his personal righteousnesses (Isa. 64:6). And that righteousness of the law of which Paul had once been so
proud, and which he considered as great merit and gain,
he came to regard as refuse (Phil. 3:4-9).

Acknowledging Jehovah's righteousness, the Old Testament saints at the same time acknowledged their own guilt. "O Lord, righteousness belongeth to thee, but unto us confusion of faces . . . to the men of Judah, and to the inhabitants of Jerusalem, and unto all Israel . . . because of their trespass that they have trespassed against thee . . . because we have sinned against thee" (Dan. 9:7, 8). The Old Testament makes it abundantly clear that a righteousness acceptable to God is impossible of attainment by man alone because of inherent sin. "The heart is deceitful above all things, and it is exceedingly corrupt: who can know it?" (Jer. 17:9, A.S.V.). "Behold, I was brought forth in iniquity; and in sin did my mother conceive me" (Ps. 51:5, A.S.V.). "How then can man be righteous before God? Or how can he be clean that is born of a woman?" (Job 25:4). And the word for man here denotes frailty, weakness.

Jehovah, who is perfectly righteous, cannot overlook this lack of righteousness in man. For He "will by no means clear the guilty." These words follow that remarkable expression of His desire and purpose to forgive sin and transgression found in Exodus 34:6, 7. "I will not justify the wicked" (Exod. 23:7). The sinner is regarded as guilty in God's sight. The soul that sinneth shall die; the wages of sin is death. And it is clear that none is capable in himself of a righteousness acceptable to God. It is obviously impossible for a fallen creature to rise to the standard of a perfect obedience. "It is quite impossible that any man can in himself be right who does not render pure, perfect, perpetual, and personal obedience to the precepts of God's law, since it is inconceivable that God could be satisfied with less."[1] How

---

[1] Whitelaw, *Jehovah-Jesus,* p. 94.

then can man be acquitted of his unrighteousness and become righteous before God?

Only Jehovah has provided such a righteousness for man. It was clearly understood by the spiritually discerning even in Old Testament times that such a righteousness must be provided by God Himself. "Surely, shall one say, in Jehovah have I righteousness . . . to him shall men come. . . . In Jehovah shall all the seed of Israel be justified . . ." (Isa. 45:24, 25). "He is near that justifieth me; who will contend with me?" (Isa. 50:8). Isaiah further predicts that no weapon formed against Israel is to prosper; every tongue rising up in judgment against her is to be condemned because her righteousness is of Jehovah (Isa. 54:17). It is this righteousness of Jehovah which the prophet further predicts is to go forth like brightness from Jerusalem, and, as the chief characteristic and glory of a redeemed Israel, will attract the nations (Isa. 62:1, 2).

But how was this righteousness of Jehovah to be applied to men? Again the spiritually minded of the Old Testament dispensation clearly understood on the one hand that the penalty of death which his sin had incurred must be borne by an innocent sufferer and that, on the other hand, the innocence or righteousness of the sufferer must be applied to him. It is only on this basis that God could declare the guilty innocent and the unrighteous righteous. Only so could Balaam understand that Jehovah "hath not beheld iniquity in Jacob, neither hath he seen perverseness in Israel" (Num. 23:21). Only so could Jeremiah say: "In those days, and in that time, saith Jehovah, the iniquity of Israel shall be sought for, and there shall be none: and the sins of Judah, and they shall not be found: for I will pardon them . . ." (50:20). For they were to be borne by an innocent one. Such an innocent person is predicted in the Scriptures.

Isaiah spoke of a Servant who should be wounded for our transgressions and be bruised for our iniquities. Upon Him Jehovah would lay the iniquity of us all and would make His soul an offering for sin. This Servant is called "my righteous servant" who should justify many by "bearing their iniquities." But who could that one be? Surely he could be no mere man, for there is no man righteous, and "none can by any means redeem his brother, nor give to God a ransom for him" (Ps. 49:7).

Apart from the fact that such a substitute and sufferer must of necessity be perfectly righteous himself and therefore more than man, the Servant of Isaiah 53 is also that Servant of Isaiah 49:7, the Holy One. He is identified by Zechariah as the Servant who is the Branch (Zech. 3:8-10). And that Branch is the righteous Branch of David and the King of Jeremiah 23:5 who is also Jehovah-tsidkenu—Jehovah our Righteousness.

"Thus while the Scriptures of the Old Testament took away from the Hebrew any hope he might have in himself, they concentrated his expectations on the living God who had specially revealed Himself to Israel."[2]

Now Israel understood that punishment for sin does not of itself cleanse a sinner, but that the righteousness of the innocent sufferer must also be reckoned to the sinner if he is to stand before Jehovah acquitted not only of penalty but of guilt. A glimpse into this marvelous doctrine of God's grace was given to men from the begin-

---

[2] Girdlestone, *Old Testament Synonyms*, p. 260.

ning. Abraham believed God and it was reckoned to
him for righteousness (Gen. 15:6). "Thou hast forgiven the inquity of thy people," 'says the psalmist, and
adds, "thou hast covered all their sin" (Ps. 85:2). And
Isaiah tells us how: "I will greatly rejoice in Jehovah
. . . for . . . he hath covered me with the robe of righteousness, as a bridegroom decketh himself with a gar-
land, and a bride adorneth herself with jewels" (61:10,
A.S.V.).

JESUS, OUR JEHOVAH-TSIDKENU

The manifestation and provision of that righteousness
of Jehovah which alone can make men acceptable to
God was fully realized in the Lord Jesus Christ, our
Jehovah-tsidkenu. In His person, character, and work
as the suffering, righteous Servant of Jehovah, He was
worthy to be substituted for Israel and for us. As the
Righteous Branch of David He identified Himself with
Israel and with us so that He could truly represent us
before God, and that in Him it could be said we have
truly met our obligations to God. Yet as Jehovah our
Righteousness He is also distinct from us so as not to be
involved in our guilt.

Jesus is Himself the Righteous One. In his great ser-
mon at Pentecost, Peter accuses his hearers of denying
the Holy One and the Just or Righteous (Acts 3:14).
Hebrews 1:8, 9 says of Him: "Thy throne, O God, is
forever and ever: a scepter of righteousness is the scepter of thy kingdom. Thou hast loved righteousness and
hated iniquity." This is a quotation of several Old Testament passages of which Psalm 11:7 reads, "For the
righteous Jehovah loveth righteousness." "He, in human

nature, lived up to the perfect standard of the divine law, so that His righteousness was of the same complexion and character as the righteousness of God."[3] Still more, as one with the Father, His righteousness was the perfect manifestation of the righteousness of God.

And then He is made righteousness to us. "Of him are ye in Christ Jesus, who of God is made unto us wisdom, and righteousness . . ." (I Cor. 1:30). And this He did on His part by paying the penalty for sin in His death for us upon the cross. "For he hath made him to be sin for us, who knew no sin; that we might be made the righteousness of God in him" (II Cor. 5:21). And Peter adds: "Because Christ also suffered for sins once, the righteous for the unrighteous, that he might bring us to God; being put to death in the flesh, but made alive in the Spirit" (I Peter 3:18, A.S.V.). What we could not do for ourselves, Christ did for us. Being Himself the Lawgiver, the Law had no claim upon Him. As perfect, He perfectly obeyed the Law for us, and became "the end of the law for righteousness to everyone that believeth" (Rom. 10:4). In His death for us as a perfect and worthy sacrifice, He took our guilt and paid our penalty.

So, on our part His righteousness is bestowed upon us as a free gift through faith. Israel's great error was in seeking to establish a righteousness of its own and in not submitting itself to the righteousness of God (Rom. 10:3). This is the great argument of Paul in Romans 3, in which, establishing the unrighteousness of man, he presents the righteousness of God as His grace in redemption toward us, closing in verse 26 with the

---

[3] *Op. cit.,* p. 269.

words: "To declare, I say, at this time his righteousness: that he might be just, and the justifier of him which believeth in Jesus." In Philippians 3:9, applying the argument to his own experience, he places all his hopes on being "found in him, not having mine own righteousness, which is of the law, but that which is of the faith of Christ, the righteousness which is of God by faith." In Romans 5, Paul argues again that as our identity with Adam brings us under sin and death, so our identity with Christ makes us the recipients of the free gift of His righteousness and life (Rom. 5:16-19).

Finally, the practical effect of the bestowal of the gift of His righteousness is to set our feet on the path of righteousness in conformity to His will whose ways are all righteousness, who loves righteousness and hates iniquity. We are to put on the new man which is created in righteousness (Eph. 4:24), and being made free from sin, we have become the servants of righteousness (Rom. 6:18).

Jehovah-tsidkenu! Wonderful name! It reveals to us the method and the measure of our acceptance before God; cleansed in the blood of the Lamb; clothed with the white robe of the righteousness of Him who is Jehovah—our righteousness—even our Lord Jesus Christ.

> I once was a stranger to grace and to God,
>   I knew not my danger, and felt not my load;
> Though friends spoke in rapture of Christ on the tree
>   Jehovah-tsidkenu was nothing to me.
>
> When free grace awoke me, by light from on high,
>   Then legal fears shook me, I trembled to die:
> No refuge, no safety, in self could I see;
>   Jehovah-tsidkenu my Saviour must be.

My terrors all vanished before the sweet name;
   My guilty fears banished, with boldness I came
To drink at the fountain, life-giving and free:
   Jehovah-tsidkenu is all things to me.[4]

---

[4] Whitelaw, *Jehovah-Jesus,* pp. 102, 103.

11

JEHOVAH-ROHI

THE NAME *Jehovah-rohi* means Jehovah my Shepherd.
It is that most precious designation of Jehovah which
begins the Twenty-third Psalm, where it is translated,
"The Lord is my shepherd." Perhaps it is not so spe-
cifically a name of Jehovah as the other names which
have been studied, but no designation of Jehovah has
brought more comfort to the heart or sounded sweeter
to the ears of the saints of both Old and New Testaments, ancient and modern, than this beautiful expression.

ITS INTRODUCTION IN THE SHEPHERD PSALM

As directly applied to Jehovah and in an intimate,
personal sense the name *Jehovah-rohi* first appears in
that immortal ode we call the Shepherd Psalm, known
and loved of all generations to this day, and perhaps
the best known of any portion of Scripture. It is the
most precious jewel in that treasurehouse of devotion,
and worship, and praise we call the Psalms. Committed
to memory in childhood's early years, it has been to
multitudes the comfort of life's closing years. It has
dried many a tear and dissipated many fears. It forms

the mold into which the faith of countless saints has been poured.

It is a psalm of David. It could not have come as appropriately out of the experience of anyone else in the Old Testament. Perhaps it was written in the latter years of Israel's great Shepherd King, the forerunner and type of that Great Shepherd of the sheep, David's greater Son. It has the ring of a full experience, of a faith sobered by trials, and a life mellowed by the passing years. He looks back upon the stormy, troubled years when his life was hunted by the inveterate enemy Saul; then through the years of warfare and rebellion, of sordid sin and sorrow; and he finds God's goodness and guiding presence through it all. Then recalling the occupation of his own childhood and youth, that of caring for his father's sheep, he can find no more beautiful and fitting analogy of Jehovah's relationship to himself than that of a shepherd to the sheep. And now after the storm and stress of the years through which Jehovah has so safely and successfully brought him, with confident faith he can look forward to the years ahead and say: "Surely goodness and mercy shall follow me all the days of my life."

MEANING AND USE OF "RO'EH"

The primary meaning of this word is to feed or lead to pasture, as a shepherd does his flock, and thus it is frequently used. The story of Joseph in Egypt opens with Joseph "feeding the flock with his brethren" (Gen. 37:2). In Egypt his brethren answer Pharaoh's inquiry by saying: "Thy servants are shepherds, both we, and also our fathers . . . thy servants have no pasture for their flocks" (Gen. 47:3, 4). "David went and returned from Saul to feed his father's sheep at Bethlehem" (I Sam. 17:15).

The word is also used figuratively to indicate the relationship between prince and people: the tribes of Israel say to David: "Thou wast he that leddest out and broughtest in Israel: and the Lord said to thee, Thou shalt feed my people Israel, and thou shalt be a prince over Israel" (II Sam. 5:2). Even of Cyrus, king of Persia, Jehovah says: "He is my shepherd, and shall perform all my pleasure," with regard to Jerusalem and the Temple (Isa. 44:28). As between priest or prophet and people, Jehovah promises to give them "pastors [or shepherds] according to mine heart, which shall feed you with knowledge and understanding" (Jer. 3:15). Contrast Jehovah's condemnation of the false shepherds through Ezekiel. "Son of man, prophesy against the shepherds of Israel . . . and say unto them, Thus saith Jehovah Elohim unto the shepherds; Woe be to the shepherds of Israel that do feed themselves! should not the shepherds feed the sheep?" (Ezek. 34:2, 8, 10).

It is used figuratively with regard to folly and judgment. The mouth of fools is said to feed on foolishness (Prov. 15:14). The idolater in his folly is said to feed on ashes (Isa. 44:20). Ephraim with its lies and deceit "feedeth on wind," says Hosea (12:1). Jehovah will feed the false shepherds with judgment (Ezek. 34:16).

It is further translated "companion" or "friend" expressing the idea of the intimacy of sharing life, food, etc. It is the word for companion in Judges 11:38 where Jephthah's daughter went away with her companions to bewail her fate. These were no doubt her most intimate, perhaps household, associates. It is the word for friend in Exodus 33:11 where "Jehovah spake unto Moses face to face, as a man speaketh unto his friend." Thus it signifies to associate with, take pleasure in, to cherish as something treasured. This is touchingly and beautifully brought out in the parable of Nathan the prophet in which he accuses David of the black crime concerning Uriah and Bath-sheba (II Sam. 12). In this parable the prophet speaks of Bath-sheba as a lamb which a poor man nourished up in his own house, which grew up with him and his children, eating of his own morsel, drinking of his own cup and was to him like a daughter.

JEHOVAH, THE SHEPHERD OF HIS PEOPLE

It is in the name of Jehovah-rohi that this relationship finds its highest and tenderest expression, for Jehovah is the Shepherd of His people. No other name of Jehovah has the tender intimate touch of this name. The name *Elohim* revealed God to us as the triune Creator and Sovereign of the universe, of life, and of all nations. As Jehovah, He was seen as the eternal, self-existent God of revelation and especially as the God of His covenant people. The name *El-Shaddai* revealed Him as the mighty, sufficient, and satisfying One. As Adonai, He was seen as our sovereign Lord, the Master of our lives and service. *Jehovah-jireh* revealed Him as the One who provides the sacrificial lamb of our redemption. *Jehovah-rophe* revealed Him as the Healer of life's sicknesses and sorrows. In *Jehovah-nissi* He was seen as the standard of our victory in life's conflicts. As *Jehovah-M'Kaddesh* He sets His people apart for His own peculiar possession and to His holy service. As *Jehovah-shalom,* He is the God of our peace. And as

Jehovah-tsidkenu He Himself is that righteousness to
His people which alone is the basis of their justification
and acceptance.

It may be clearly seen then that none of these names
can mean quite the same to His people as this precious
name. It is a wonderful and beautiful conception when
we consider the general picture of Jehovah presented
thus far in the Old Testament. He is awful and unap-
proachable in His holiness. Not even Moses may see
His face or look upon the fullness of His glory, for no
man can see that and live (Exod. 33:20). At best
Moses can endure only a passing glimpse or manifestation of it. Jehovah is sublime in His purity and glorious
in majesty, whose thoughts and ways immeasurably
transcend the thoughts and ways of His people (Isa.
55:8, 9). Yet the wonderful grace of Jehovah as expressed by the word *shepherd* is such that He can con-
descend to such a relationship with mortal, sinful creatures, whom He has redeemed.

The psalmist and the prophets are the first to apply
this name of Jehovah. It appears first directly and personally in the Twenty-third Psalm. Everything in David's life had suggested such a relationship. On one great
occasion God had said to him, "I took thee from the
sheepcote, from following the sheep, to be ruler over
my people" (II Sam. 7:8), and the psalmist adds: "He
chose David . . . to feed Jacob his people, and Israel his
inheritance. So he fed them according to the integrity of
his heart" (Ps. 78:70-72).

Thereafter this designation of Jehovah appears frequently. "Give ear, O Shepherd of Israel, thou that
leadest Joseph like a flock . . ." says the psalmist (80:1).
In that great chapter of comfort, Isaiah 40, of the mighty,

sovereign God the prophet says: "Behold Jehovah Elohim will come with strong hand. . . . He shall feed his flock like a shepherd: he shall gather the lambs with his arm, and carry them in his bosom, and shall gently lead those that are with young" (vv. 10, 11). Ezekiel also gives us a beautiful picture of this relationship in 34:11-16, where after the indignation at the false shepherds Jehovah is presented as the Shepherd who will search His sheep and seek them out. He will feed them in a good pasture and make them to lie in a good fold. He "will seek that which was lost, and bring again that which was driven away, and will bind up that which was broken, and will strengthen that which was sick."

The Scriptures give us some intimate glimpses into the life of the shepherd and the sheep, but fortunately the preservation of this relationship to this very day enables us to better understand all that Jehovah may mean to us as Shepherd. A recent traveler in Palestine observes: "Shepherding does not change much in Palestine where wild beasts may descend still upon unprotected sheep and suddenly destroy them. The Palestine shepherd lives night and day with his animals. He establishes a degree of intimacy with them which is touching to observe. He calls them all by their names and they, knowing his voice and hearing his only, heed. He protects the sheep from thieves and preying animals who would devour them at night, by sleeping in the opening of the often makeshift sheepfold and they, sensing his watchfulness, fear 'no evil.' He provides pasture and water even in the wilderness and the presence of enemies and they, casting all their anxiety upon him, are fed. There is a singular communion between the shepherd and his sheep which, after one has visited Palestine and observed it, makes the symbol of the good Shepherd peculiarly apt and the Twenty-third Psalm strangely moving."[1]

It is wonderful that Jehovah should be all this to His people. How well Jacob understood the ceaseless vigilance and constant exposure required in a shepherd! He speaks of that which was torn of beasts and that which was stolen of robbers. In the day the drought consumed him, and the frost by night, and the sleep departed from his eyes. His experience seems to him but a shadow of the loving care, the watchful protection, the strong defense of God, "the God who fed me [or shepherded me] all my life long" (Gen. 48:15). So Jehovah, as the psalmist so beautifully puts it, is the Keeper of His people—their shade upon their right hand. He does not allow the sun to smite them by day nor the moon by night. He keeps them from all evil. He who keeps His people neither slumbers nor sleeps (Ps. 121). We are reminded of the attachment and devotion to the sheep in the risking of the shepherd's life to protect them from perils and pitfalls, by David's own exploits in rescuing them in single, unaided combat from the very mouth of the lion and the bear, so that the combat with a Goliath seems a small thing by comparison. The shepherd must be resourceful, resolute, strong. Jacob calls Him "the mighty God . . . the shepherd" (Gen. 49:24). And as we have seen, Isaiah says of Him: "Behold the Lord God will come with strong hand. . . . He shall feed his flock like a shepherd. He shall gently lead. . . ." The shepherd is both strong and gentle.

Everything that the shepherd is to the sheep, Jehovah

---

[1] Patterson, *Around the Mediterranean with My Bible*, pp. 142, 143.

is to His people. If there can exist such a tender intimacy between a man and sheep, how much more so between Jehovah and the spirits He has created and redeemed; and what a marvelous thing that God should offer Himself for such a relationship. He had said, "I will dwell among the children of Israel" (Exod. 29:45), and the word *dwell* is the word *Shekinah,* denoting His glorious presence. Jehovah as Shepherd offers His people the intimacy of His presence. He may be as intimately known as the shepherd is of the sheep. Poor sheep indeed are they who do not know the shepherd as they should, for his voice will not be so familiar and they will not follow. Such go easily astray. This was Israel's tragic experience, who were "the sheep of his pasture" (Ps. 100:3), but who became scattered and were as "sheep that have no shepherd" as the prophet foresaw in vision (I Kings 22:17). The intimacy of the shepherd is the most precious privilege and possession of the sheep, and this the Lord's people, as His sheep, should cultivate and enjoy. But it comes only by long and constant association and abiding in His presence.

Jehovah-rohi is not only the Shepherd of His people, He is my Shepherd, the Shepherd of each one of His people. As the God of the individual He was intensely personal. Not that Israel indulged in vague philosophical speculation or pantheistic dream about Jehovah, but every one of His flock and of His fold could say, "I am the Lord's and he is mine." They understood that He had each one of them in mind. Each one could say, "Thou knowest my downsitting and mine uprising" (Ps. 139:2). The psalm is full of personal pronouns. It is the psalm of personal experience with a personal God to whom every sheep of the fold is precious and His particular care. Since its experiences are common and its emotions familiar, we may claim it each one for himself.

JESUS OUR SHEPHERD

Of all the names of God in the Old Testament none is more beautifully pictured and personified in the New Testament than the name *Jehovah-rohi,* in the person of that glorious Shepherd of the sheep—the Lord Jesus Christ. Some of the most beautiful and appealing of His parables and sayings have to do with this relationship to His redeemed. There is no more familiar and tenderer association concerning Him than that of the Shepherd going after the sheep that was lost. In no other delineation of Him do we feel more of His grace and beauty, His strength and gentleness than in that great shepherd discourse of John 10. The glorious announcement of His birth was first made to shepherds keeping watch by night over their flock, happy omen of what He was to become to men. And His last injunction to Peter before ascending to sit at the right hand of God the Father is to feed and tend His sheep.

"I am the good shepherd," He said (John 10:11). Surely those who heard Him could not have mistaken His meaning. He was the "I am" of Isaiah 40:11, the Lord Jehovah who was to come as a mighty One and to feed His flock like a Shepherd and gently lead them.

In Him was fulfilled the word of Ezekiel: "For thus saith the Lord Jehovah: Behold, I myself, even I, will search for my sheep, and will seek them out . . . I will deliver them . . . I will feed them with good pasture . . . I will cause them to lie down . . . I will seek that which was lost, and will bring back that which was driven away, and will bind up that which was broken, and will strengthen that which was sick" (Ezek. 34:11-16).

His shepherd heart was melted with compassion for a people who were like sheep without a shepherd, and wrung with grief for the scattered sheep of the house of Israel, whose Shepherd He was. He would have rescued and gathered them (and will yet), but they would not. He is the "great shepherd of the sheep" of Hebrews 13:20. And Peter reminds us that we were going astray like sheep but have returned to Him who is the Shepherd and Bishop of our souls (I Peter 2:25).

He qualified Himself to become that good and great Shepherd by first becoming a lamb, thus entering intimately into every experience and need of the sheep. "For verily he took not on him the nature of angels: but he took on him the seed of Abraham" (Heb. 2:16). He partook of our flesh and blood (Heb. 2:14), so that as "he himself hath suffered being tempted, he is able to succor them that are tempted" (Heb. 2:18). He is touched with the feeling of our infirmities, for He was tempted and tried in all points as we are, yet without sin (Heb. 4:15). He Himself learned obedience and was made perfect through sufferings (Heb. 2:10). For as a lamb, He subjected Himself willingly to the Father's will, when "it pleased Jehovah to bruise him" and to "make his soul an offering for sin" (Isa. 53:10), so that while all we like sheep had gone astray, Jehovah laid on Him the iniquity of us all. For He was led as a lamb to the slaughter (Isa. 53:6, 7) and He bore our sins. Thus He was able and worthy to become that good Shepherd of the sheep, under which figure also He gave His life for the sheep (John 10:11).

As the Shepherd He has gone on before and prepared the way, for having offered one sacrifice for sins forever He sat down at the right hand of God (Heb. 10:12), and we have boldness to enter the holy place by His blood, the new and living way He has dedicated for us (Heb. 10:19, 20).

As the good and great Shepherd of the sheep He meets every need of His flock (Phil. 4:19), and there is no want to those who trust him. He leads us into the green pastures of His Word, and feeds us upon the true Bread of Life. He guides us into right paths and we are assured of His continuous presence. The Spirit of truth, He promised, will guide you into all truth (John 16:13). "I will pray the Father," He said, "and he shall give you another Comforter, that he may abide with you forever" (John 14:16). For the Shepherd and the sheep are never separated. By day He gently leads, and by night He is the door of the sheep (John 10:9, 10). He protects us from the perils that beset us round about, and our perils are very real. Paul at Miletus warned the elders of the Ephesus church: "For I know this, that after my departing shall grievous wolves enter in among you, not sparing the flock" (Acts 20:29). "Beware of false prophets, which come to you in sheep's clothing, but inwardly they are ravening wolves," explained the Shepherd Himself (Matt. 7:15). From these false teachers who exploit and destroy faith, and from the poisonous plants which the sheep may eat, and from the pitfalls of error into which they may wander, the abiding presence of the Spirit of truth will keep us.

There were not only wolves and pitfalls for the sheep. There was another significant danger from which the shepherd protected them. As he went ahead his eye was ever on the alert for the snakes whose sting was death, and with his staff he would crush their heads. So the great Shepherd, who has already sealed the serpent's doom, will deliver us from falling into his power. We are safe in the protection of His table spread before us even in the presence of the enemies. He knows every one of His sheep by name. He knows the particular need of each one of us. He knows our peculiarities. He knows our weaknesses. Do we know His voice as we should? Do we trust Him and follow Him as we should? Is there the beautiful intimacy between us that there should be? Do we love the Shepherd's presence? Can we distinguish His voice from the voice of the wolf in sheep's clothing who comes among us to wrest and wreck our faith?

And when we are sorely tried He will lead gently on. When we are weary and wounded He will anoint our heads and heal our wounds and refresh us with tender care. As His sheep we are led by many a way. Sometimes the path is through fresh green meadows; sometimes over rough, steep, rocky paths, perhaps through dark places where the sun scarcely shines. But we are ever being led to one place. After the heat and burden of the day, He gathers us into the fold, where there is no more fear of wolf or thief and where all is sweet repose and safety. And then we know that whatever the sufferings and sorrows, the trials and terrors of the day, His goodness and lovingkindness followed us.

So the Lord Jesus, our Jehovah-rohi, will lead us into that final fold and rest "before the throne of God" where, John says, "they serve him day and night in his temple: and he that sitteth on the throne shall spread his tabernacle over them. They shall hunger no more, neither thirst any more; neither shall the sun strike upon them, nor any heat: for the Lamb that is in the midst of the throne shall be their shepherd" (Rev. 7:15-17, A.S.V.). So we "shall dwell in the house of Jehovah forever."

12

JEHOVAH-SHAMMAH

AND THE NAME of the city from that day shall be, Jehovah-shammah" (Ezek. 48:35).

The meaning of the name *Jehovah-shammah* is Jehovah is there. In the light of its setting and significance it is a most fitting name with which to climax the Old Testament revelation of God. By His various names Jehovah had revealed Himself in the power and majesty and glory of His person and as meeting every need of that man whom He had made in His image and for His glory. His name *Elohim* revealed Him not only as Creator and Ruler, but as covenanting to preserve His Creation. The name *Jehovah* revealed Him in special relationship to man. For since that name indicates absolute self-existence, and therefore One who is infinite and eternal, it could be revealed only to creatures who could apprehend and appreciate the infinite and eternal. And since the name *Jehovah* sets God forth in His moral and spiritual attributes, the special relationship between Him and the crowning work of His Creation, the man made in His image, was a moral and spiritual one. That moral and spiritual relationship was broken by man's disobedience and sin and fall. After that, the names of God compounded with Jehovah reveal Him as providing redemption for fallen, sinful man, and depicting every aspect of that great transaction of redemption by which man is fully restored to God—healing, victory, peace, sanctification, justification, preservation, care, and guidance. Jehovah-shammah is the promise and pledge of the completion of that purpose in man's final rest and glory, for man's end is to glorify God and enjoy Him forever. For, as Paul says, "Whom he did predestinate, them he also called: and whom he called, them he also justified: and whom he justified, them he also glorified" (Rom. 8:30), a past tense, but speaking the language of eternity.

THE OCCASION OF THE NAME

The name *Jehovah-shammah* is found in the last verse of the Book of Ezekiel. Ezekiel began his prophecies at a time when the nation Israel was at the lowest ebb of its history, spiritually and nationally. The sun of its strength and glory had long set, and the night was fast closing in. Every one of his prophecies was uttered in captivity where he had been taken several years before the destruction of Jerusalem. The last great vision and prophecy was uttered in the twenty-fifth year of the captivity and fourteen years after Jerusalem had fallen, the Temple destroyed, and only a poor, miserable remnant left in the land. Israel's spirit was broken, and Ephraim's crown of pride was laid low in the dust. It appears they had been delivered from bondage in Egypt only to go into bondage in Babylon. By the rivers of Babylon, the psalmist tells us, they sat and wept, as they remembered Zion. Song had departed from them. They hung their harps upon the willows. "How shall we sing Jehovah's song in a strange land?" they answered their captors when they demanded of them one of the songs of Zion. In the land of their humiliation and sorrow they had time to reflect upon their follies and to realize the pleasantness of their heritage now laid waste and the beauty of Jehovah's sanctuary now destroyed. Then they vow: "If I forget thee, O Jerusalem, let my right hand forget her cunning. If I do not remember thee, let my tongue cleave to the roof of my mouth; if I prefer not Jerusalem above my chief joy" (Ps. 137:5, 6).

Perhaps with the passing of the years, or with the easing of the conditions of captivity, enthusiasm for Zion was beginning to wane. At any rate, the Ezekiel who twenty-five years before had prophesied to the early captives in Babylon the destruction of Jerusalem and the Temple, now brings this prophecy of hope and consolation which predicts the restoration of land and people in a measure far beyond anything they had ever experienced in the past, or could have imagined. The pledge of all this is the name *Jehovah-shammah,* Jehovah is there.

The Jehovah who had departed from the old Temple, desecrated by the abominations of His people (Ezek. 10:18, 19; 11:22-24) and destroyed by His judgments, now returns by the same way into a new and glorious city and Temple, purged of all the old abominations and oppressions, and characterized by righteousness, justice, and holiness. The glory of Jehovah would fill this new place, and His presence would dwell and abide there forever (Ezek. 43:1-7). Ezekiel heard a voice saying to him: "Son of man, this is the place of my throne, and the place of the soles of my feet, where I will dwell in the midst of the children of Israel forever." All this vision Ezekiel was commanded to take back from Jerusalem, where he had been taken in spirit, to the captives in Babylon, for their heartening and hope.

THE MEANING OF THE NAME

The uniqueness and glory of Israel's religion as contrasted with the religions of the surrounding nations had always been the presence of a holy God dwelling in their midst. The condition of His continued presence among them was to be their faithfulness to a covenant by which they promised to be a holy people to this holy God. This again was in striking contrast to the surrounding nations whose worship was as cruel and licentious as their gods.

Jehovah had promised His presence among His people from the beginning. Whatever the outward symbols or manifestation, the Presence was real and felt. "Behold, I send an Angel before thee, to keep thee in the way, and to bring thee into the place which I have prepared," He said to Moses (Exod. 23:20). In verse 23, this angel is "my Angel." He is the angel of Jehovah who appeared to Moses at the burning bush (Exod. 3:2), and who announces Himself to Moses as the "I am that I am"—Jehovah Himself (Exod. 3:14, 15). In answer to Moses' plea to continue with His people in spite of their great sin and provocation, Jehovah says: "My presence shall go with thee, and I will give thee rest." And Moses continues: "If thy presence go not with me, carry us not up hence. For wherein shall it be known here that I and thy people have found grace in thy sight? is it not in that thou goest with us?" (Exod. 33:14-16). Moses reminds the children of Israel as they are about to enter the Promised Land, "because he loved thy fathers, therefore he chose their seed after them, and brought thee out with his presence" (Deut. 4:37, A.S.V.). And in a wonderful passage of Scripture, Isaiah remarks: "In all their affliction he was afflicted, and the angel of his presence saved them: in his love and pity he redeemed them; and he bare them and carried them all the days of old" (63:9). In a beautiful psalm, which tells of David's desire and purpose to build a house for Jehovah to dwell in, we read: "Arise, O Jehovah, into thy rest; thou, and the ark of thy strength. . . . For Jehovah hath chosen Zion; he hath desired it for his habitation. This is my rest forever: here will I dwell; for I have desired it" (132:8, 13, 14).

Both tabernacle and Temple were the place of His abode and His visible manifestation in Israel. The New Testament makes it quite clear that these Old Testament edifices were figures of the true, the pattern of things in the heavens (Heb. 9:23, 24). Everything about them was highly typical of God's presence and glory. Of their free and willing gifts the children of Israel erected these costly and beautiful buildings. As soon as the tabernacle in the wilderness was completed and dedicated, we are told that the glory of Jehovah filled it, and the cloud of Jehovah was upon the tabernacle by day, and there was fire therein by night, in the sight of all the house of Israel, throughout all their journeys (Exod. 40:34-38).

David desires to build a "house" for Jehovah to dwell in because all these centuries since they had first entered the land Jehovah had "walked in a tent and in a tabernacle" (II Sam. 7:5-7). And when that magnificent Temple was built by his son Solomon on the very site of Mount Moriah, where Jehovah had revealed Himself to Abraham as Jehovah-jireh, a great and dramatic scene ensued. At the end of Solomon's great prayer of dedication, the fire, fitting symbol of Jehovah's presence and power, came down from heaven, consumed the sacrifices on the altar, "and the glory of Jehovah filled the house. And the priests could not enter into the house of Jehovah, because the glory of Jehovah had filled Jehovah's house" (II Chron. 7:1-3).

The fullness of Jehovah's presence was the hope and end of all prophetic expectation. After the glorious prophecy of Messiah's universal reign in the eleventh chapter, Isaiah pens a beautiful psalm of praise in chapter 12 which ends with the words: "Cry out and shout, thou inhabitant of Zion: for great is the Holy One of Israel in the midst of thee." Also speaking of a future fulfillment, Jeremiah says: "At that time they shall call Jerusalem the throne of the Lord" (3:17). "Glorious things are spoken of thee, O city of God," says the psalmist of Zion (Ps. 87:3). Of the city trodden under foot and despised, Isaiah says: "They shall call thee The City of Jehovah, The Zion of the Holy One of Israel" (60:14). In Psalm 46, that great psalm of confidence, Jehovah is represented as "the indwelling Helper." Here mention is made of "the city of God, the holy place of the tabernacles of the most High. God is in the midst of her. . . . The Lord of hosts is with us; the God of Jacob is our refuge." Whereas all about in the earth is turmoil and tumult, war and ruin, there is safety, security, tranquility, in the city of Jehovah's constant presence.

But to return to Ezekiel's vision and prophecy, was the fullest meaning of the name *Jehovah-shammah* to be realized in any earthly habitation? "Will God," asks King Solomon on the very occasion of the dedication of the Temple, "will God in very deed dwell on the earth? Behold, heaven and the heaven of heavens cannot contain thee; how much less this house that I have builded!" (I Kings 8:27).

The orthodox Jewish interpretation of this vision has always been a strictly literal one. Its fulfillment is to be realized in an earthly Jerusalem, a temple rebuilt and the sacrificial system restored. Then Messiah is to come and reign as the Son of David with Jerusalem as His throne and the spiritual and political center of the earth. So Jehovah-shammah is realized.

Some Christian interpreters have also supported the view of a strictly literal interpretation and as having no other significance. Others have interpreted the vision only in a typical, spiritual sense, as having no literal fulfillment whatever in an earthly Jerusalem and a restored, national Israel. There are still others who combine the two interpretations and declare that the vision has both a literal fulfillment and a wider, spiritual and final fulfillment. Israel will indeed be restored to their land and resume their worship. Messiah, the Prince, will indeed appear for their salvation and the setting up of His kingdom when every knee shall bow before Him and every tongue confess Him as Lord. But there is an even fuller, a final application to be made of this prophecy, that of a new heaven and new earth wherein dwelleth righteousness, a home eternal in the heavens. For it is quite obvious that even though Ezekiel was bidden to carry this vision back to Babylon for the hope and encouragement of the captives there, it had a much larger significance than could ever have been realized by their return. And as a matter of fact, nothing in the program of this vision was adopted by them when they did return.

THE FULFILLMENT OF THE NAME

It has been seen that the fulfillment of this name was limited in the Old Testament both in its manifestation and scope. Every manifestation of God's presence in the midst of His people, though real, could only be but a shadow of a glorious reality to come. As to its scope, it was limited to the nation Israel.

In the New Testament dispensation it has a wider scope in that it is more spiritual than symbolic, and more personal rather than national. For now it has been fulfilled ideally in the person of the Lord Jesus Christ.

As man and representing the human race "the whole fullness of God was pleased to dwell in him" (Col. 1:19, marg.). He was the effulgence of God's glory and the very image of His substance (Heb. 1:3, A.S.V.). "The Word became flesh and tabernacled among us," says John, "and we beheld his glory" (John 1:14). Thus He became "God with us," the Immanuel of Isaiah 7:14, the Child, the Son, the mighty God, the everlasting Father of Isaiah 9:6. The One who in the Old Testament came in occasional, mysterious appearance as the Angel of Jehovah, the Angel of His Presence, the Angel of the Covenant, the Angel in whom is Jehovah's name, became in Christ both the Presence itself and the Temple in whom the Presence resided so that in Him and of Him it could be said Jehovah-shammah, Jehovah is there.

This Presence is now in believers as living temples of God. "Know ye not that ye are a temple of God, and that the Spirit of God dwelleth in you" (I Cor. 3:16). "What agreement hath a temple of God with idols?" Paul further says to the Corinthians: "For ye are a temple of the living God; even as God said, I will dwell in them, and walk in them; and I will be their God, and they shall be my people" (II Cor. 6:16).

Like Israel of old, the Church as a whole, as the Body of Christ, is also called the habitation of God. Of the true Church it can be said, "Jehovah is there." Speaking of the Gentiles, Paul calls them no more strangers but fellow citizens together with believing Jews, with the saints, and of the household of God, built on the same foundations of apostles, prophets, and Christ the chief cornerstone. He describes it as a building fitly framed, growing into a holy temple in the Lord, a habitation of God in the Spirit (Eph. 2:19-22). Christ promised His abiding presence to His Church (Matt. 28:20), being present even where two or three should be gathered in His name.

It will certainly have a larger fulfillment yet for Israel in a millennial kingdom. Of a restored Israel and Palestine, where every man shall dwell safely under his own vine and fig tree, when the mountains of the house of Jehovah shall be established (Mic. 4:1-6), and Messiah, The Branch, the beautiful and glorious Branch of Jehovah, shall build the temple, and bear the glory and rule as prince and priest upon His throne, with counsels of peace (Zech. 6:12, 13), there can be no doubt unless the plainest prophecies are so spiritualized as to rob them of all sense and understanding, and destroy the meaning and integrity of prophecy.

But, as already indicated, the name *Jehovah-shammah* has a final and eternal fulfillment. This was intimated by the Lord Jesus in His parting discourses to His disciples. He spoke about the many mansions in His Father's house from which He would return to take His disciples to Himself that they should be with Him there (John 14:2, 3). "Father, I will that they also, whom thou hast given me, be with me where I am; that they may behold my glory" (John 17:24).

The ideal of life even in the Old Testament was never conceived of as being fully realized on earth. "As for me," says the psalmist, "I will behold thy face in righteousness: I shall be satisfied, when I awake with thy likeness" (Ps. 17:15). "My flesh shall rest in hope," for "in thy presence is fullness of joy; at thy right hand there are pleasures forevermore" (Ps. 16:9, 11). And the New Testament declares that our "citizenship is in heaven" (Phil. 3:20).

The ideal and future life was often pictured under the figure of a city. Even the psalmist must have had in mind something of what Ezekiel saw in his vision, something more than the earthly Zion he knew, when he wrote: "There is a river, the streams whereof shall make glad the city of God, the holy place of the tabernacles of the most High" (Ps. 46:4). The great cities of the world are built on the banks of broad, deep streams, but Jerusalem had no river. It is an ideal, a heavenly Jerusalem in which this saying finds its final and fullest realization. Abraham looked for a city which had foundations, whose builder and maker is God (Heb. 11:10). He saw the final fulfillment of the promise "afar off." He desired a better country than any earthly Canaan could be, that is, a heavenly country, as his true home, for he confessed himself a stranger and pilgrim on the earth (Heb. 11:13-16). The writer of the Epistle to the Hebrews tells us: "Ye are come unto Mount Zion, and unto the city of the living God, the heavenly Jerusalem, and to innumerable hosts of angels, to the general assembly and church of the first-born who are enrolled in heaven" (Heb. 12:22, 23, A.S.V.). And of that city the Book of Revelation says that there was no temple there. There was no further need of any outward symbol of Jehovah's presence, "for the Lord God, the Almighty, and the Lamb are the temple thereof" (Rev. 21:22).

The ideal and eternal character of this city of God, the place of His full and glorious presence, finds its most sublime expression in Revelation 21 and 22. "I saw a new heaven and a new earth: for the first heaven and the first earth are passed away; and the sea is no more. And I saw the hoyl city, the new Jerusalem, coming down out of heaven from God, made ready as a bride adorned for her husband. And I heard a great voice out of the throne saying, Behold, the tabernacle of God is with men, and he shall dwell [or tabernacle] with them, and they shall be his people, and God himself shall be with them, and be their God" (Rev. 21:1-3). In that beautiful city, foursquare with its precious stones, its crystal river, its delectable fruits, and tree of life with its leaves for the healing of the nations, all will be light, and love, and holiness, and worship, and joy, and safety. There shall be no more curse, no adversary, no defilement, no sorrow, for every wicked doer shall be cut off from that city of the Lord or Jehovah. Then will be realized the full and final rest of the redeemed, the Sabbath rest of creation restored. The glory of Jehovah will be fully manifested in the Lamb that was slain. He will be seen and known in the full meaning and beauty of all the names by which He had revealed Himself to man's imperfect apprehension. And we shall join in saying "unto him that sitteth on the throne, and unto the Lamb be the blessing, and the honor, and the glory, and the dominion forever and ever" (Rev. 5:13).

Read all of the *Names of Series*